BHANUDAS

Monumenta Indica Series No. 7

BHANUDAS

The Poet-Saint of Maharashtra

Translation from the Bhaktivijaya

Justin E. Abbot

Sri Satguru Publications
A Division of
Indian Books Centre
Delhi - India

Published by:
Sri Satguru Publications
Indological and Oriental Publishers
A Division of
Indian Books Centre
40/5, Shakti Nagar,
Delhi-110007
(INDIA)

First Edition: Poona, 1926
Second revised Edition: Delhi, 1996

ISBN 81-7030-498-9

Printed at
D.K. Fine Art Press (P) Ltd.
Delhi 110052
Printed in India

CONTENTS

APPENDIX

PREFACE

TO

POET-SAINTS OF MAHARASHTRA SERIES.

I have long felt that the stories of the Maraṭha saints, which tradition has handed down, were a valuable moral asset, not only to the people of Mahārāshṭra, the home of those saints, but to all India.

At present these stories are not easily available, for the reason that the Maraṭhi language and literature are hardly known outside of Mahārāshṭra. Even in Mahārāshṭra little prominence is given to the interesting and suggestive lives of those Maraṭha saints who by their godly and righteous lives have been a blessimg to Mahārāshṭra. I am not unmindful of the eflorts made by Mr. L. R. Pāngārkar, Mr. D. B. Sàhasrabuddhe, and others to popularize the lives of the Maraṭha saints, but their writings have all been in the Maraṭhi language, and, being untranslated, are not available for those who do not know that language. To make these stories of the Maraṭha saints available to a large circle, both in India and outside, an English translation is obviously a necessity. And as I feel that these stories have a moral value, and that they can be used to impress vital truths, the translation of them into the English language has been for me a labour which I have felt was worth while, and has been a labour of love.

Those who have not dipped into Maraṭhi literature are naturally unaware of the original sources of the stories of the saints which are current in Mahārāshṭra. I have therefore made it my task to translate the original sources, from which all consciously or unconsciously draw, when they pass these stories on to others, either orally, or in written form.

It is to Mahipati, who was born, lived, and died at Tāhārābād, in the Rāhuri taluka of the Ahmednagar District, that the chief glory belongs for collecting from manuscripts, and perhaps somewhat from oral tradition, the stories of the old saints, and recording them in his own graphic style in his Bhaktavijaya, Bhaktalilāmṛita, Santavijaya, and Santalilāmṛita. Some of the original sources from which he obtained his information are still extant, but for the most part we are dependent on Mahipati alone for any extended knowledge of those saints. Were it not for him, the lives of even such saints as Eknāth and Tukārām would be unknown except in a very meagre way. All honour therefore to Mahipati, to whom Mahārāshṭra and the world owes a heavy debt of gratitude. Aside from Mahipati there are lesser lights that have recorded the traditional stories of some of the saints. While some are older than Mahipati, some are almost plagiarists from Mahipati, and some have evidently another and independent source. Altogether there is a considerable body of literature which can be considered original sources. They are the oldest we possess, and it is to such that I have turned for the English translations which I have made.

In connection with these original sources, it should be observed that if in modern books, or on the lips of men, there are stories of these saints that differ in detail from those of the original sources, they are undoubtedly due to misquotations. The possibility of an independent source for these deviations may be conceded, but it is so improbable that very strong evidence would be needed to establish the fact of such an independent source. We all know that Indians are good story tellers. Some are professional story tellers. Deviations from the original sources may therefore be only from the love of embellishment or from the slip of memory, but if their history be tracted the seeker will without doubt be led to the original sources extant in manuscript or printed form.

From the above it becomes evident why I have confined myself to the stories of the Marāṭhā saints, as found in the oldest sources or in the nearest removed from them, for the basis of my translations. They are nearest to the times in which those saints lived, and the traditions recorded in these oldest accounts are as near to the truth of their lives as we can at present arrive. No eye witness accounts of the lives of those saints exist, except that in some of their works these saints have left us slight references to their own lives, their ancestry, their religious teachers. In the case of Tukārām, his abhangs furnish much information regarding the chief events of his life, corroborating some at least of the traditions recorded by Mahipati. Another unique exception is the autobiography of Bahinābāī, in which not only is her early life described, but several important references are made to her actual meeting with Jairām Swāmi, a disciple of Rāmdās, and with Tukārām at Dehū, and others. But these eye witness accounts are very meagre, and the traditional accounts, written in most cases centuries after those saints really lived, are all we have to acquaint us with the lives of those godly men.

Dates.

The dates generally assigned to the births and deaths of the Marāṭhā saints are very uncertain. No one has yet undertaken a thorough and scientific study of the question. Some of the most universally accepted dates stand on very insecure foundations. Generally the easy method of following tradition has been pursued. As the subject now stands, one does not know what to accept as historic facts regarding their births and deaths, and what as mere guesses, however wise some of them may be. It is much to be desired that some competent scholar would undertake this problem, and in the place of the present confusion, present all the available facts, making it possible to discriminate between solid facts and wise guesses.

As I have not attempted to do what must fall to the lot of some more competent scholar, I feel that it will be less confusing if I accept as the probable dates of the Marāṭhā poet-saints, those assigned them by such scholars of Marāṭhī literature as Mr. V. L. Bhave, L. R. Pāngārkar and others. For the purpose of these translations the subject of dates is a comparatively minor one, and it is more fitting for me to accept the verdict of the experts I have mentioned, than to indulge in my own guesses, unless impelled by very strong evidence. Where the experts disagree I shall have to choose, as best I can, the dates that seem to me to be upheld by the best authorities.

The above observations naturally bring me to the question of how far these traditional accounts can be trusted for a true picture of the lives of those saints. I cannot agree with a certain school that divides the traditional accounts into two categories, the possible and the impossible. The possible, that is, stories that conform to our ordinary life and the ordinary laws of nature, are called history, while the impossible, that is, the miraculous element, are called myths. I do not agree to this division, for, on the one hand, good story tellers can embellish their stories with additions, or a faulty memory can do the same, and these may be quite in harmony with our ordinary human life. The fact that they are classed as possible events cannot make them history. This thesis can be easily proved. For example, Mahipati's account of Eknāth in his Bhaktavijaya, written in 1762, differs in several important details from the fuller account of Eknāth in the Bhaktalilāmṛta, written in 1774, twelve years later. Some of these details are contradictory. They are in the class of the possible, but that fact cannot be trusted for accuracy. Stories passed down from mouth to mouth through centuries can vary as much in the probable as in the improbable events that they record. That which is called mythical, because miraculous, because not conforming to the ordinary laws of nature, some would put aside as not historical. This I regard as a great mistake, for the reason—and the proof of it can be given—that the mythical form given to a story may be only the embellishment of a later period. The kernel of it can be in the class of the possible, and hence can be history. Hence, since we have no eye witnesses, and since there is no way of corroborating these stories, the question of their exact historic value may well be set aside, except in those cases where there are corroborating evidences from eye witnesses. These, however, are unfortunately very few.

What then is the value of these stories, if we cannot be sure what details are true, and what the embellishment and additions made by story tellers up till the time when they were recorded by Mahipati and others many years after those saints lived? There is much value in them, and fortunately that value does not depend on the historic basis of those stories. A moral truth can be as impressive, whether seen illustrated in the record of an event that actually took place, and that can be proved by the strongest evidence to be history, or whether seen illustrated in stories whose historic basis is uncertain, because of the distance of time, and the accidental non-existence of corroborating eye witnesses. A moral truth stands on its own feet, and is not dependent for its value on the accidental history in which it appears, be it in a historic writing or in fable.

These stories of the Marāṭhā saints have great moral value in that they give us pictures of Godfearing, righteous men, who in their lives sought to honour God, and to live for the good of their fellowmen. Aside from these stories, there are their own poetic works, which not only mirror their own inner thoughts, but corroborate the stories of their lives by their teachings. So that it has seemed to me a task well worth while, to make these Poet-saints of Mahārāshṭra better known to India, to the world, and even perhaps to the Marāṭhā people themselves, through an English translation of original sources, with comments that a study of them for many years has made possible for me.

I am well aware that these translations will have readers who will regard them from different points of view. Because these stories of the saints are so largely religious, those to whom religion is a vital matter, will naturally look at them, and weigh them, from their special standpoint. But I think there is one point of view from which we can see them alike. We can see those saints, where at Āḷandī Paiṭhan, Dehū, Paṇḍharpur, or Paraḷi, with physical surroundings very much as they are to-day. We can see them brought up from childhood by parents or *gurus* in perfect faith in the religious and philosophic beliefs current in Mahārāshṭra in their day. They were loyal to those beliefs. They believed in the divine origin of the Vedas, the Upanishads, the Mahābhārata, the Rāmāyana, and the Purāṇs.

The Puranic stories were not myths to them, but sober history. The Vedanta philosophy was the backbone of their thinking, like the spine of their bodily frame. Their reasoning, and the general conduct of their lives, were in harmony with their beliefs. They were not critics of those beliefs, but their interpreters. The reader may agree, or violently disagree, with their philosophic and religious beliefs, but when it comes to the stories of their lives, as they seem to have lived them, they are seen to be godly men, revering and honouring God according to their conception of Him. In their relation to men, and in the struggles with their own inner life, they may not appear to all as perfect examples, but they were examples, nevertheless, of those who loved the good, the pure, the kind, and the true. The reader may not approve of all they may have said or done, but he will be a blind reader if he cannot look behind those words and deeds and see hearts that wished to say and do what was right, and good. And when the reader, whatever his religious or philosophic beliefs may be, compares his own private life with those of these Marāṭhā saints, he will find in them many a helpful thought, and inspiration to a nobler life.

It has been the custom of some to use these stories and the teaching of these Marāṭhā saints in the way of comparison with the life and teaching of other saints and teachers. Such comparison is perfectly legitimate in its place. Truth, which is what we should all seek for, is often arrived at through the path of comparison. I can, therefore, foresee that the readers of these stories will use them in different ways, and one will be that of comparison. But I as firmly believe that the scholar in his study of these saints in his comments on their lives and teaching, in his translations of the old records, should not let his personal philosophic and religious beliefs appear. The reader has a right to presuppose that the present writer has presented his subject in as impartial a way as may be possible for him. The later use of the material gathered, and recorded, is quite another thing. There personal opinions and points of view have a legitimate place. This I believe is the only right and true way for a scholar, and it is the reader's right to demand this impartial dealing with these historic subjects.

In accordance with the above I have sought to be as accurate as I could in my translations, as exact as the materials in my possession have allowed me, and as impartial as possible in my comments on the lives of these Marāṭhā saints. It sometimes falls to the lot of a translator to hesitate about some story or some expression because to his reader it might seem indelicate. But no such difficulty has yet met my path. Mahipati, and indeed all the other writers on the Marāṭhā saints, have stories only that are pure, and I have therefore had to use no expression that would bring a blush to the most sensitive cheek. The lives of those saints were pure lives, and whatever liberties tradition may have taken in embellishing or adding to their tales, the impure has found no place.

It is but fair to the reader to confess to the difficulties under which I labour in producing these translations and comments. I am in America, with no pandit at my side to help me over difficult points of text, of meaning or of idiom. My knowledge of Marāṭhī, is, I feel, painfully deficient, in spite of the fact that it began when I was four years of age, and that its study covers practically all my life, with perhaps special opportunities through a long life among the Marāṭhā people. The serious task of making these translations has made the above fact evident to myself. It will be still more evident to those Marāṭhī scholars whose language it is, and whose knowledge of the subject is so much more perfect than mine. But I feel as Mahipati felt. He felt himself inadequate to the task of properly presenting the lives of these saints, yet he was sure of the sympathy of his audience, through their sharing with him the love of these saints. I also have learned to love these poet-saints of Mahārāshṭra, and in making this offering of English translations—flowers, may I call them—to the people of Mahārāshṭra, I know them too well not to know that they will accept these flowers with the kindness, the courtesy, the sympathy, and the love which is so characteristic of them, not only because they are offered, but because of their own love for their old poet-saints.

How many numbers will appear in this series I cannot say. That depends on the life which may be still mine. I am seventy-two years of age. Body and mind are in good health, but the limit of life is approaching. I would like to live ten years more, provided body and mind keep their health. That length of time would enable me to cover a large ground, and make the result of my many years of study available to those who may not have had the time to make independent research. But, however many or few may be the remaining years of my life, I offer them to Mahārāshṭra, where most of my life has been spent, and whose saints of old, and whose people to-day, I love.

I begin the series with Bhānudās, the great grandfather of the great and noble saint, Eknāth. It will probably be followed by the Life of Eknāth. I am not planning any particular order in which I shall present these saints. That will depend on the material I have in hand, and the progress of my study. Where the lives are short I am planning to print with the translations the original Marāṭhī text. Where, as in the case of Eknāth's life, the account is long, the addition of the Marāṭhī text would not be practicable.

On account of the distance from India, the difficulties connected with the publishing of these translations would have seemed insurmountable, had not Dr. Nicol Macnicol of Poona, who needs no introduction to the Marāṭhā people, offered to see them through the press. I owe him a great debt of gratitude for this kindness.

It is but fitting that I should here acknowledge my debt of gratitude to Mr. V. L. Bhave, author or *Mahārāshtrā Sārasvata,* to Mr. L. R. Pāngārkar, to Mr. S. S. Deva, Mr. V. K. Rajvade, Mr. D. V. Potdar, and many others, who have done such valiant service in Marāṭhī literature, and to whom I owe so much. To them I make my *namaskār.*

JUSTIN E. ABBOTT.

Summit, N.J., U.S.A.,
FEBRUARY 10, 1926.

BHĀNUDĀS.

INTRODUCTION.

Original Sources of Information.

The Marāṭhā poets who have made Bhānudās the subject of their song are:-

Viṭṭhalkavi of Bīḍ, about A.D. 1679, who relates the story of how Bhānudās brought back the image of Viṭhobā from Vidyānagara.

Keśav swāmī, about 1682, who relates the story of how the image of Viṭhobā was taken by Rāmrājā to Vidyānagara, and how Bhānudās brought it back.

Mahipati in his Bhaktavijaya, which he completed in 1762, who relates the story of the birth of Bhānudās, his childhood, his unwilling but successful mercantile life, his becoming a *sannyāsi,* the events that led to Rāmrājā's taking away the image of Viṭhobā to Vidyānagara, and its return through Bhānudās.

Mahipati in his Bhaktalilāmṛita, which he completed in 1774, relates the story of Rāmrājā's removal of the image of Viṭhobā to Vidyānagara, and its return through Bhānudās. This he draws largely from the account of Keśavswāmī, mentioned above.

Bhīmaswāmī Śirgāvkara, in 1797, who covers the same ground as the Bhaktavijaya account, except that he begins with the mercantile life of Bhānudās.

Eknāth, 1548 to 1609, the great grandson of Bhānudās. In his Bhāgavata, chap. 1, 130-132, and in his other works, he makes short references to his distinguished ancestor, corroborating some of the traditional stories recorded in the Bhaktavijaya. (See Eknāthāchi Abhangāchī Gāthā, Indu Prakasha Edition of 1906, p. 70 A 2, 9-12; p. 102 A 36, 48; p. 106 A 79, 4; p. 121 A 51, 9; p. 198 A 20, 3; p. 199 A 28, 3; p 470 line 27). (See also Swātmasukha by Eknāth, line 506). (See also Sukāshtaka by Eknāth, line 438).

Other Marāṭhā poets mention Bhānudās in an honoured way, but give no information regarding him.

Moropant in his Sanmaṇimālā; Nīlobā (see Nīlobāchi Gāthā 1557, 148); Nāmdevāchī Gāthā, abhangs 361 and 775. See also Dāsodigambarkrita Santavijaya, prasang 7; Santamālikā by Uddhavachidghana, 44; Santamālikā by Jayarāmasuta (Mahārāshtra Kavi No. 9, p. 8); Santamālikā by Śivarām (Mahā. Kavi No. 9, p. 9); Santanāmāvalī by Rangnāth (M.K. 9, p. 11); Santamālikā by Siddhachaitanya (M.K. 9, p. 13); Santanāmāvali by Bahinābāī (Bh. I.S.M. 17, p. 77); Ganeśgītā by Bhagavān Karhāḍkar (Bh. I.S.M. 9, p. 157); Rāmavarada by Mukund (Saṅkirṇalekh Saṅgraha, p. 19); Santamālikā by Eknāth (Saṅkirṇalekha Saṅgraha).

The Interrelation between the above Original Sources.

The solemn assertion of Mahipati that he had not drawn on his imagination for the stories of the Saints, but had drawn from the writings of others should be noted. In his Bhaktavijaya 1.37-39 he says, "You may perhaps say that I have written this book out of my own imaginations and conceptions, but this truly is not so. Have no doubts about this. In the northern country one Nābhāji, an avatār of Brahmadeva, wrote a very large book, called the lives of the Saints (Santacharitra) in the Gwālheri language. One Uddhavachidghana of Māṇdesh also wrote a book called

Lives of the Bhaktas (Bhaktacharitra). Combining these two I have begun this Bhaktavijaya."

In his Santalilāmṛita, written to complete the stories omitted in his Bhaktavijaya, 1.67-69, Mahipati says, "You may raise a doubt in your mind and say he has drawn on his own imagination. This is not so. Listen. Great poet-saints have written books in many languages. It is on their authority that I write this Santalilāmṛita. If I wrote on my own authority my accounts would not be respected. The Husband-of-Rukmiṇi, who knows all hearts, is witness to this."

A like assertion is also made in his Bhaktalilāmṛita 1.167-170, and one cannot question the honesty of Mahipati in his use of what he considered authorities. Compare also Bhaktalilāmṛita 10.169-174, where his faithful following of written documents is again asserted, his slight additional embellishments being compared to the good housewife who adds a little water to the fresh milk that it may suffice for her whole family.

The works of Nābhāji and Uddhavchidghana may have been an inspiration to Mahipati to commence his Bhaktavijaya, but their works, as we know them to-day, are too meagre to have been of any value to him in his detailed account of the many saints of whom he wrote. His information therefore must have come from the many other books which were extant in his day. It would not be safe to say that Mahapati did not draw from oral tradition in some cases, but that that was not his ordinary method is clear from his own definite statements, and from the results of a critical examination of his works.

Turning now to his account of Bhanudas, and that of Viṭṭhal Kavi and Keśavswāmi, it is clear that all three originate in a common source, in the form of a written document. That original source is, either, now not extant, or is yet to be found, in some private collection of manuscripts. It was probably written, somewhere midway between the death of Eknāth (1609), and the poet Viṭṭhal Kavi, who made use of it. The above statement is of course an hypothesis, but one that, if true, clears away difficulties connected with the relation of the different original sources to one another. With this hypothesis, the relation of the several accounts, may be graphically represented as follows :—

Bhānudās

Oral Tradition

A Bhānudās charitra, work and author unknown,

Viṭṭhal Kavi about 1679

Keśavswāmi about 1682

Mahipati in Bhaktavijaya 1762

Mahipati in Bhaktalilāmṛita 1774

Bhimāswāmi Śirgāvkar about 1797

The unknown Bhānudās-charitra, suggested above in my hypothesis, was probably a part of an Eknāthcharitra, that also being now unknown. Mahipati used it in his Bhakatavijaya account of Eknāth, as Keśavswāmi had also done before him. But Mahipati in his Bhaktalilāmṛita, seems to have regarded Keśavswāmi a better authority, so that in his Bhaktalilāmṛita account of Eknāth, Mahipati draws his information from that source. This hypothesis provides a needed key for the explanation of the differences in important details between the account of Eknāth in the Bhaktavijaya and that in the Bhaktalilāmṛita. When Keśavswāmi's text and that of the Bhaktalilāmṛita are placed side by side the reader can have no doubt as to Mahipati's source for his Bhaktalilāmṛita account of Eknāth. It is to be hoped that, this now unknown source from which Mahipati drew his Bhaktavijaya account, may yet be discovered. Could the author be Mukteśwar, grandson of Eknāth, whose Śri Khaṇḍyākhyāna, may have been a part of a now non extant Eknāthcharitrá?

BHĀNUDĀS.

Date of birth and death, about 1448-1513.

As Mahipati's account of Bhānudās in the Bhaktavijaya is practically all that is known of the events of his life, the date of his birth and death are mere wise guesses. From Eknāth's own writings we know that Bhānudās was his great grandfather. He also informs us that Bhānudas died at the time of the birth of his grandson Suryanārāyaṇa, the father of Eknāth. (Eknāthi Bhāgavata 1.130-134). If the usually accepted date of Eknāth's birth is assumed to be 1548, then Mr. Pāngārkar's guess (Eknath charitra p. 21) that Bhanudas died in 1513 may be provisionally accepted. So also 1448, as the date of his birth, may be provisionally accepted, since his life covered two generations, which would be allowing 65 years as the span of his life. These dates are also given by Mr. Bhave in his Mahārāshṭra Sārasvata, 1st Ed. p. 100, note. They are, however, only wise guesses.

Information additional to Mahipati's account.

From *Eknāth* (Eknāthī Bhāgavata 1.33) we learn that Bhānudās lived until the birth of his grandson Suryanārāyaṇa. Eknāth speaks of him as of a family line "loved of God." Hence we may assume that he was born into a religious and pious family.

Bhimaswāmi Shirgāvkar adds two stories in his account of Bhānudās not found in Mahipati's account. These stories in substance are :—

1. In the straitened circumstances in which the wife of Bhānudās found herself, God appears in human form and supplies the household with food and money

sufficient for the rest of their lives. Bhānudās immediately gives away all his property to Brahmans.

2. Bhānudas, feeling that the god, Viṭhobā, was ill disposed towards him, adopts a ruse, which ends in reconciliation.

At the end of Bhimaswāmi's account of Bhānudās and Eknāth, he says that what he has written is from what he heard from the lips of the saints. This may be interpreted to mean oral tradition, which would perhaps more easily account for his deviations and his frequent anachronisms.

Are the stories about Bhānudās history of fiction?

As has been observed in the general preface to this series, there have been no accounts from eye witnesses, with one exception, of the lives of these Marāṭhā saints. First oral tradition, and then tradition in oral and written form, is the form in which we know their lives. Very little light is thrown on them from contemporary history, which is exceedingly meagre. Oral tradition by additions and embellishments can make a man's life appear very different from what it was, even if the stories are in harmony with man's ordinary life. On the other hand, because a story is told in a form that appears like fiction, it does not mean that there may not be a historical fact at the basis of it. Examples can be furnished of a tradition appearing in two forms, the one fitting in with ordinary human life, the other in a setting in which the miraculous appears. The difference, therefore, may not be in the historic value of the story, but in the way of telling it.

In reference to Bhānudās in particular, we have the small amount of information given by his great grandson

Eknāth. This may be well taken as history. All the rest which we gather from tradition falls under the second category of a possible historic basis, but of this there is no evidence, for or against.

The attempt to find a historic basis for the story of Bhānudās bringing back from Vidyānagara the image of Viṭhobā, has not been as yet successful.

Bhānudās as a Poet.

A collection of the Gāthās of the Marāṭhā poet-saints has been made by Mr. Tryambak Hari Avate, and published by the Indira Press, Poona, under the title Sakalasantagāthā, in 1924. In referring to the abhangs of Bhānudās I shall for convenience use this edition. In this collection there are 94 abhangs ascribed to Bhānudās. Neither in this edition, nor in previous ones, does Mr. Avate give any information as to the manuscripts on which the printed editions have been based. Opportunities for textual criticism are, therefore, lacking, and the question of the genuineness of each *abhang* as being the work of Bhānudās, must for the present be an open one. *Abhang* 78 cannot be by Bhānudās, as it shows an acquaintance with the traditions connected with his great grandson Eknāth. *Abhangs* 90, 91, 92, give in concise form the miraculous deliverance of Bhānudās at Vidyānagara. If these three *abhangs* are really by Bhānudās, they would have great historic value. There is room for just suspicion that they are not by him. A few of the *abhangs* in this collection are quoted not only by Mahipati, but long before him by Keshavswāmi, showing them to be a part of a collection of abhangs ascribed to Bhānudās, and well known, at that early date. Modern editors of Marathi texts have done a great disservice to Marathi literature in taking *abhangs* out of their original order, as found in the manuscripts, and arranging them according to subject matter. This has made confusion worse confounded in the case of the text of Tukārām's *abhangs,* and the same is true here of the *abhangs* of Bhānudās. The science of textual criticism has not yet been applied to the texts of the poet-saints.

Assuming the genuineness of these *abhangs* as a whole, Bhānudās appears

Firstly, as an intense devotee of God, as represented to him in Viṭṭhal of Paṇḍharpur. Before the idol of Viṭṭhal he sang and danced. But to Bhānudās, Viṭṭhal meant God as he manifested himself to the saint Puṇḍalik long before, and now still manifesting himself in deeds of love and mercy. That he identified Viṭṭhal with the Supreme Being is seen by the epithets he uses, such as, "Life of the World" (74), "Creator of the Universe and the Ruler of all living things."

Secondly, as emphasizing the moral character of God, he speaks of God's impartiality. "It is my experience that God does not turn away from a suppliant, be he king or subject, be he of noble family or an outcaste" (47). To him God was a forgiving God. "O God, forgive all my transgressions" (64). A Saviour, "Has it come to thy thought that I should descend to Hell? I, a poor sinner, have come to thee for refuge. Somehow carry me safely. I am helpless, hear my petition. I, Bhānudās, would sing thy praise" (61). God is called Father and Mother, "Thou, Father and Mother, are the Saviour of the universe" (27), (71). "God is a loving being," (66). "God is merciful," (70). God is Saviour of the sinner. "I am a fallen, fallen sinner. Thou art my saviour, O eternal Lord" (69), (72). God is "the helper of the helpless" (68).

Thirdly, in philosophy Bhānudās appears as a Vedantist, but he gives little space to its metaphysical side. His interest centres in the *saguṇ* Iśvara, God conceived as a personal being, and especially as one who in frequent *avatārs* has made himself very close to needy humanity, as saviour (27, 69, 71, 72), helper (68), and friend (53). Though God, with qualities, understandable by men, (saguṇ), is identified with "the Eternal Brahma" (74), with "the Brahma described in the Vedas" (10), it is the *saguṇ* Iśvara, manifested in the various avatars, and especially dear to him in His manifestation as Viṭṭhal at Paṇḍharpur, that excites Bhānudās' enthusiasm. As a Vendantist, Bhānudās was a rigid monotheist. As a traditionist, he wholeheartedly accepted the theory of the Supreme Being, being both, *nirguṇ* and *saguṇ,* without qualities, and yet with them. All *avatārs* were of the one *saguṇ* God, and to be indentified with one another. Viṭṭhal, Rām and Hari, were but the names of those manifestations of God, which at different times and under different conditions, made himself known and felt as the Saviour and helper of man.

Fourthly, Bhānudās' moral point of view. Necessity of a clean life. "Unless there is felt the defiling nature of the desire of another's wealth or another's wife, there can be no pure religious life" (45). He bemoaned the fickleness, and sensual tendencies of his own heart. "My heart is so fickle! I cannot restrain it. It is pestered by sensual desires. The power of wrong thought has become tremendous. The six enemies of the soul attack me from all sides. The power of right thinking has become weak, and the will to do what is right has disappeared. O Hari, Thou who pullest the strings of human thought, have mercy on me, Bhānudās" (60). Of himself as a sinner he often speaks, "Because I am a sinner, I have come as a suppliant" (67). "I am a sinner and a wrong doer" (81), (69). All the requests that Bhānudās made of God were spiritual requests. Of worldly things he had no desire. "I will not engage in the painful business of providing for my body. Do Thou satisfy my hunger from what may be left over from the favours given to others" (77). "Of giving and taking I want no more. My desires have been satisfied" (69). "As the bumble bee seeks the pollen, as the bee seeks the honey, so my heart seeks this God, Pāṇḍuraṅg. Says Bhānudās, take me to Paṇḍhari, and make of me a glad offering to Viṭhobā" (19). "A transgressor in all things, I, a fallen sinner, come to Thee as a suppliant. Do not turn me away. Says Bhānudās, fulfil my desires, O Pāṇḍuraṅg, helper of the helpless" (59).

The English translation of Mahipati's account of Bhānudās.

In the following translation of Mahipati's account of Bhānudās, as given by him in the Bhaktavijaya, chapters 42 and 43, I have endeavoured to be as literal as possible, consistent with the usage of the English language. In some cases I have had to be less literal, and less idiomatic, for the translator has to meet serious difficulties arising from a large number of causes. With all its possible defects, I trust that, this story in its English dress, may awaken a wider interest in this Marāṭhā poet-saints. And if this should take place, I shall feel myself fully rewarded for the labour which I have so gladly put upon it.

Aside from interest in the story of Bhānudās, I trust that there may be aroused greater interest also on the historic and textual problems, for it may yet be that there are hidden away in private collections, or in *maṭhs,* manuscripts not yet available, but which, if found, might throw additional light on this early Marāṭhā saint, who lived four hundred years ago.

Translated from Bhaktavijaya, Chapters 42 and 43.

INVOCATION.

1. Obeisance to Śri Ganeśa. Obeisance to Śri Kṛishṇa. Victory! Victory to Vāsudeva, Lord-of-the-Earth Lotus-eyed one, Husband-of-Rukmiṇi, Giver-of-happiness-to-his-Worshippers, without whom there is no happiness. 2. Victory, Victory to Him of the Lotus-navel, whose form is the Universe, Father of the Creator, Lord-of-Heaven, Radiant-of-form, Dwarf-shaped, Indescribable-by-Vedas-or-Śastras. 3. Victory to Thee, Unlimited-universal-arm, the all-seeing-eye, He-who-fills-universal-space, Thou who hast spoken in the words of the Vedas. 4. O Thou-whose-form is Radiance, Lord-of-the-senses, because Thy worshippers cannot fully know Thee, Thou didst take a *saguṇ* form, and set them to worshipping Thee. 5. O Lord-of-Lakshmi, Thou becomest to them whatever they desire, just as a mother, of graceful carriage, leads her child along, holding it by the hand. 6. Her heart rejoicing in the sweet prattle of the little lisper. She speaks back to it in the same pratling way, kissing it in her love. 7. The same thing happens to Thy bhaktas, who, lacking knowledge, praise Thee in foolish, babbling words, and Thou, Life-of-the-world, in Thy loving mercy makest Thyself as simple to them.

THE BIRTH AND BOYHOOD OF BHANUDĀS

8. In the last chapter there was recorded the deeply interesting story of the life of Mṛityunjaya, in which you, Hearers, became absorbed, as you listened. Such is the infinite glory of the Saints.

9. Now it happened that the Ṣun already manifested himself as an avatār at Pratishṭhāna. And I would that

you, a good people, would listen with loving attention to the following interesting story. 10. To a wise, holy, and pious Brahman, a worshipper of the Sun, there was born the treasure of a son, to the great delight of his heart. 11. Day by day the boy increased in stature. In due time the ceremony of the sacred thread was duly performed. His father and mother bestowed on him boundless love.

12. It happened one day that in assigning him the task of studying the Vedas, the father showed anger. From fear of that anger the boy sulked. 13. He left the house. He made great efforts to find a place in which to conceal himself, and at first failed. But suddenly in his wandering his eye fell on a deserted temple. 14. This temple lay hidden under ground. People did not visit it, so the boy at once entered and remained there in hiding. 15. There was an antique image of the Sun in that temple, and the boy at once prostrated himself lovingly at its feet. 16. Seeing the boy's devotion the Sun was pleased, and said to himself "Although this child is ignorant, his heart has firm trust in me." 17. The Sun then assumed human form, and approached him. He gave the boy all the milk he could drink, and gave him the assurance of his protection from all fear. 18. He said to him, "Let your heart be without fear. Keep Śri Pāṇḍuraṅg in your remembrance. If you should ever fall into any distress, at your call I will immediately be present with you."

19. Turning now to the father and mother, who with sad hearts were searching for their son, it happened that seven days passed, and yet they had not found him. 20. But one day the Brāhman's son stepped outside the temple. There happened to be there one of the Twice-born, and he spied the lad. 21. He called out to him, but the boy

at once ran back into the temple. The Brāhman then came into the town and related the event to the father. 22. The father and mother rejoiced to think that their son had been found, and taking some of their townspeople with them started to find him. 23. There in the forest they discovered to their surprise a deserted temple. They lighted torches and bravely descended into it. 24. As they entered, they all saw the image of Nārāyaṇa, and the Brāhman's son sleeping with his head on the feet of the image. 25. The father and mother bent over their son, and drew him to their lotus-hearts, exclaiming, "How has it happened that you have survived in this place, all alone?" And tears flowed from their eyes. 26. The people then asked him, "How have you kept yourself alive here? For your hunger and thirst you surely could not obtain food here." 27. He replied, "A supremely glorious, radiant Brāhman has appeared to me here. He has fed me with milk, and thus saved my life." 28. Hearing these words of the child, all marvelled, exclaiming, "Evidently seeing the child's trust and devotion, Suryanārāyaṇa has manifested Himself to him." 29. And it was because the Sun had manifested this delight in the boy, that he was given the name of Bhānudās (Slave-of-the-Sun). The parents taking him on the hip returned to the town. 30. They remarked to one another, "It is God who has saved his life. Let us forbear speaking to him in harsh words. Nārāyaṇa, in His mercy, has given us this gift of a son. 31. Whatever events are fated to occur they will take place in time. Why should we needlessly distress his heart." 32. Thus comforted in mind, the parents let affection govern them. "We will not assign him the task of acquiring knowledge," they said, "lest he should again sulk and leave us." 33. They now made search for a bride, and had Bhānudās married. But in the passing days Bhānudās devoted himself entirely to the worship of Śri Hari.

BHĀNUDĀS BECOMES AN UNWILLING PEDDLER OF CLOTH.

34. When the allotted life of Bhānudās' parents had come to an end they passed away. Bhānudās, however, without concern for consequences was unwilling to engage in any worldly occupation. 35. He would serve no one for remuneration; he would engage in no trade or commercial dealings; he would have no borrowing or lending of money; he refused ever to enter the king's service. He wished only to be occupied with the worship of Pāṇḍuraṅg. 36. There was need, however, in his home for food and clothing. His wife moreover was distressed in mind. And although he had children, yet he lived indifferent to all worldly needs. 37. A few men of influence, however, came together to speak to Bhānudās on his affairs. "Your wife needs food and clothing," they urged, "but you seem unable to comprehend this. 38. While your father and mother were living they bore on their own heads the burden of your worldly necessities. But what is going to happen in the future, if your mind continues indifferent to these things? 39. It is also true that you have not acquired much learning. Hence we make you a certain proposal. Let your ear listen to it with respect. 40. We will supply you with a hundred rupees in cash. Buy cloth and peddle it. 41. From the profit you gain, you will be able to provide your family with food and clothing. Carefully preserve the principal and return it to us gradually as you may find it convenient."

42. These men then went to the market, purc ased cloth and handed it over to Bhānudās. These men had

other peddlers under them, and Bhānudās was committed to their care. 43. "When you go to the market-place take him along with you," they said. "Seat him at your side, and put him in the way of gaining his livelihood." 44. The peddlers listened to the words of the men and consented. They took Bhānudās with them, and seated him beside them. 45. They taught him their secret numerical code: mulu (five), udanu (three), angolu (ten), kevala (one), kaṭhi (twenty), pavitru (seven), 46. selu (six) poku (four), dhakār (one thousand), āvāru (two), and other numerals. They explained to him about the cloth, and how to sell it. 47. How one should carefully protect the principal, and what pains should be taken to tell a price that would yield a profit. How also if one tells the exact truth, one will certainly meet with loss. 48. To this last advice Bhānudās replied, "I will never, so long as time lasts, speak an untruth. I will speak only the absolute truth." 49. At this all the peddlers laughed. "It is evidently written on his forehead that he must live by begging," they exclaimed. "This explains why it is that he will not listen to anything we say. His name should rather be 'Poorman.' " 50. One cynically remarked, "Let him once get the taste for gain. Then he will utter falsehoods in plenty. One has never seen any one favoured by Fortune, who speaks the truth in his business relations." 51. How true it is that one who is born blind thinks that all men are blind. Even savory food seems bitter to one bodily sick. 52. So it is that the man who is false in heart, sees no one true. As a man's heart is, so others seem to him.

53. But Bhānudās showed great courage. He refused to utter any falsehood in his business. The result was that every one marvelled at it, and people flocked to his stall. 54. If a customer asked him about the cloth, he would tell

him the exact cost price to him, and the profit he was asking on the principal. He gave them but one answer. 55. "If you approve of it take it. If not, pass to another stall." This is all he would say to them, and then continued his repeating of the names of God. 56. And all came to recognize the truth that God does fill man. "Bhānudās will never even to the end of time speak an untruth," they declared. 57. Customers appreciating his truthfulness all came to him. The other peddlers, dishonest in their dealings, had to watch the marvel from where they were. 58. They began to murmur, "That we have given him a place beside us has been to our injury." And hatred now arose in the hearts of these evil doers. 59. "He sits beside us and draws away to himself our customers," they cried. "(Hypocritically) we look him boldly in the face, but within we burn with rage to no avail." 60. Another remarked, "He throws a spell on people. That is why they have become bewitched. They pay down the price he asks, and no one even haggles over it." 61. Still another observed, "People have come to believe in him, and that is why they patronize him. We are untruthful. We are the slaves of worldly desires. And God does not approve of this." 62. Finally one said, "Let us now speak the truth." To this another objected, saying, "Though we should do so, no one would regard us now as really worthy of confidence. 63. Once character is fixed it continues the same through life. This we see exemplified in Bhānudās before our very eyes. 64. A dog may be sitting quietly in the house. Thieves may come and steal away the bread. The accusation, however, will fall on the dog, for no one could know by intuition who really took it. 65. A tiger may be lying down peacefully, but it will be said he is crouching to spring and kill. A miser may become an ascetic, but it will be said that he has started out on a course to deceive. 66. An adulterer may indeed visit sacred watering places, but it will be said that he is in search of others' wives. A cat may be lying perfectly quiet, but people will remark that it is looking for a rat. 67. So it is with us. Our whole life has been spent openly in the sight of others, speaking untruths. And now, though we should act with honesty, people will say, 'This is useless hypocrisy.' 68. Bhānudās began before our very eyes with a very small business in cloth, and now he has become a prosperous man. God has been his helper. 69. We make great effort, but we are unable to obtain sufficient bread to satisfy our appetites. Our creditors come and sit at our doors. What are we to do? 70. Ever since we gave Bhānudās a place beside us we have become bankrupt. He has drawn away all our customers, and we are now in distress."

BHĀNUDĀS TURNS AWAY FROM WORLDLY AFFAIRS.

71. One day all those peddlers started on their way to a distant market place. Their journey ending, they put up in a temple precinct. 72. Bhānudās, the Vaishṇava bhakta, had also come along with them to that market place, and as usual had placed his stall next to theirs. 73. Now it happened that a Haridās had come to that same town, and had arranged for a kīrtan that very evening. An invitation had been passed around the town that all should come to the recital. 74. When Bhānudās heard of this, he was filled with great delight. "To-day is an auspicious day, the eleventh of the moon," he exclaimed, "I must go and listen to the kīrtan." 75. Bhānudās invited the peddlers to go with him to the kīrtan. (As they refused) he said

to them, "If, because of laziness, you are unwilling to come with me, you will at least be sleeping beside our wares. 76. So protect my stall, and care for my goods with yours." This request of Bhānudās made them very angry. 77. "You have become God-crazy," they sneered. "You are forever telling the truth. Now go to this Hari recital, and take your goods along with yourself. 78. We are all wearied, and are going to sleep. Seek some other place for your stall, where you can display your wares. 79. There are thieves around here, and we wish for no words of blame from you. We cannot understand what gain is going to fall into your lap from going to this kīrtan." 80. Bhānudās replied, "Well, let my goods remain here or be stolen, (I care not). My heart is fixed on Pāṇḍuraṅg. I will never desert him." 81. Thus remarking, Bhānudās, the Vaishṇava bhakta, left his goods as they were and hastened away, soon reaching the place where saints were gathered to listen to the kīrtan. 82. With his heart full of joy he made a *namaskār* to the Haridās, "Happy is this occasion," he said, "the eleventh of the moon." He then embraced the saints. 83. The Vaishṇava sang lovingly the Rām and Kṛishṇa stories that bring salvation to mankind. Bhānudās listened with great delight, for he had a great love for them.

84. In the mean while the evil minded peddlers sat beside their wares and planned as follows. "Bhānudās has left his wares here and has gone to the kīrtan. 85. Let us therefore play a trick on him. Unknown to him we will let his pack-horse go loose, and throw his bundle of cloth into a ditch. 86. When he comes back to ask us about it, we will say, 'Thieves came while we were in deep slumber, and stole it without our knowing of it'. 87. He will then go back to his own home, and we can then divide the cloth here among ourselves." Having thus planned, these evil

men let his pack-horse go loose. 88. There was a deep pit near by, and into it they threw the bundle of cloth. They clapped their hands over the deed, and said to one another, 89. "Since Bhānudās has been with us he has acquired wealth, while we have become poor. All customers go to him. 90. Now all our anxiety is gone. Without the use of medicine the itch has disappeared." In this manner these evil men talked the matter over among themselves. 91. Just as Duryodhana rejoiced in his heart when he robbed Dharma of his wealth, so these evil minded peddlers rejoiced in their hearts.

92. But when the Husband-of-Rukmiṇi saw the calamity which had befallen Bhānudās, He immediately arrived on the scene, saying to Himself, "Bhānudās is sitting listening in the kīrtan in fixed contemplation. 93. These evil minded men have conspired together and thrown his wares into the pit. What plan shall I follow," said the Life-of-the-World to Himself. 94. His pack-horse will wander away somewhere. Where will he then look for it? He has put aside fondness for worldly things and gone mad after my worship." 95. Thus thinking to Himself, Paṇḍharināth assumed the form of a Brāhman. Finding the pack-horse near the market-place, he sat down holding it. 96. He who reclines on the serpent in the Ocean of Milk, He on whose feet Lakshmi meditates, He who espouses the cause of his *bhaktas,* Captivator-of-the-Heart, He sat, holding the horse. 97. He who does not come quickly even into the mental conception of the Yogis as they sit in meditation; He the espouser of the cause of his *bhaktas,* Lord-of-the-organs-of-Sense, He sat, holding the horse 98. He, Śriraṅga, who cannot be attained by religious rites, sacred places, austerities, or yoga, He, Pāṇḍuraṅg, He who gave his promise to Puṇḍalika, He sat

holding the horse! 99. He, the father of Brahmadeva, the creator of the limitless universe, caught the horse of Bhānudās as it was wandering about, and sat holding it in the public square!

100. In the mean time the peddlers were sitting in the temple precincts reviling Bhānudās. "He will soon come back to look after his wares," they said. 101. "When he hears what we tell him has happened here, he will become greatly agitated." As these villains were thus talking among themselves the Dark-Complexioned-One became very angry. 102. And while the Life-of-the-World was expressing his anger, suddenly thieves approached. They robbed the peddlers of their goods and gave all a severe beating. 103. They loosened all their pack-horses and took them all away. And now the peddlers sat weeping. "We persecuted Bhānudās" they said, "and Pāṇḍurang has made us experience the result." 104. One remarked "According to our *karma,* so are our minds. We certainly lack knowledge. We have not used forethought." 105. Still another remarked, "Fortune has played us false. Therefore we performed this loathsome act. Bhānudās is a single-minded *bhakta.* With no gain to ourselves we have troubled him." 106. They made now a loud outcry, but no one came running to them from the town. The Husband-of-Rukmiṇi skilled in the use of *māyā,* had cast a spell upon all.

107. Turning now our attention to the kīrtan, there were heard their shouts of joy. The drum and the *viṇā* gave out their sweet sounds. The air was filled with the music, while the names of God were being acclaimed aloud. 108. The night was now lacking four *ghatikās,* when the Vaishṇava sang the final hymn of praise, waving incense reverently before the Husband-of-Rukmiṇi. Sweetmeats

were then distributed. 109. Bhānudās made his obeisance to the Haridās, and started back to his lodgings. Suddenly he saw a Brāhman sitting by the wayside holding a horse. 110. As he was passing by, the horse neighed. "How happens it that my horse is here?" he said to himself. "I cannot understand it." 111. Just then the Brāhman, who had thrown his scarf around the neck of the horse, and was sitting holding it by it, saw Bhānudās, and suddenly vanished from sight. 112. As Bhānudās saw this marvel, he was overwhelmed within with wonder, but leading the horse along he arrived at his lodgings. 113. Here he found the peddlers weeping aloud. Asking them what the trouble was about, they made full confession to him. 114. "We, evil-minded wretches, sought to do you harm. We threw your bundle of cloth into yonder pit, and let your horse loose. 115. When it was the second watch of the night, thieves appeared and robbed us of our all. Now to whom shall we go and complain of the ways of destiny? 116. All our horses and bundles of cloth are stolen. We have also received a severe beating. And now it looks as though our business has come to an end. 117. We have lost all of our principal. God has protected yours. We threw your bundle of cloth in yonder pit. Let us all now go and care for it." 118. When Bhānudās heard their story his heart melted. "I think" he said, "it must have been the Husband-of-Rukmiṇi, who was sitting holding my horse. 119. Botheration! All this worldly business is without real value. It is no store-house for the happiness of the soul. Worthless wretch that I am! I have been seduced. 120. Think of it! That He, Fair-of-complexion, delicate, with the eyes of a lover, clothed in the yellow silk robe, Life-of-the-World, in the form of a Brāhman, should be sitting holding my horse! 121. No longer will I engage in a business that brought weariness to Paṇḍharināth." With this repentance in heart he then addressed the peddlers. 122. "Let your minds be at rest. Thieves have beaten you, but let not your hearts sorrow." 123. Then drawing the bundle of cloth out of the pit he distributed the pieces of cloth among them. Bhānudās further offered to them his horse and his money, and then left them.

BHĀNUDĀS BECOMES AN ASCETIC.

124. He returned to his home, and there devoted himself entirely to the worship of Hari. He put aside all thought of whether he was being honoured or dishonoured. He spent his life singing in *kīrtans* the attributes of God. 125. He refused to enter any one's service. He would not let his mind be involved in the anxieties of worldly affairs. Though he had a wife and children, yet he acted with perfect indifference to worldly things. 126. It became his custom in the months of Ashāḍh and Kārtik to lead bands of pilgrims to Paṇḍhari. On the sands of its river he would perform *kīrtans,* accompanied by cymbals, drums and loud acclamations. 127. Being gifted with the poetic art, he would compose verses in different meters and offer them as incense to the Dark-complexioned-One. His heart was a spring of love. In his *kīrtans* his voice would choke with emotion. 128. When Bhānudās stood up to perform his *kīrtans,* tears of joy filled all eyes. And the Husband-of-Rukmiṇi, seeing this love of theirs, would himself come there and dance. 129. Wicked men, evil-minded, and the ignorant, even they, as they listened, became filled with love, and would exclaim, "We could listen forever to these enlightening *kīrtans,* sung by his lips. 130. How false, indeed are the illusions of this worldly existence. How

perishable are these bodies of ours!" And as these listeners gained in knowledge, they began to love all creatures.

131. Adopting the non-begging method of the ascetic life, Bhānudās accepted such food and clothing as were voluntarily offered to him. His own lips asked nothing of any one. 132. The idea of mine and thine, had now no meaning to him. He realized the unity of all creatures, He had put aside all thought of differences. 133. Thus Bhānudās' mind was characterized by utter indifferences to worldly things. And he spent his days and nights, in the joy of his heart, in the worship of Śri Hari.

134. In the next chapter we shall listen to the story of the taking of the Saviour-of-the-World, by the king Rāmrājā, to Vidyānagara. The intelligent listener to this story will feel joy within his heart. 135. You saints and good people in this divine assembly! Mahipati stands in your presence, with a handful of flowers, in the form of Marāṭhi verses. 136. Swasti! As the Lord-of-the-Earth listens to this book, the Śri Bhaktavijaya, He also will be pleased. Loving, devoted *bhaktas* listen then to it. This is the forty-second delightful chapter. It is an offering to Śri Kṛishṇa.

CHAPTER 43.

1. Obeisance to Sri Ganes. Obeisance to the Son-of-Vāsudeva. Listen, you hearers, good and loving people. To-day the Wishing-tree has come to fruit. These intensely interesting stories of the saints are now revealed to you, enlightening and beyond compare. 2. I would have you know the indescribeable glory of Vishṇu, the limits of which even Brahmadeva does not know, and of which the

Vedas also are ignorant, a glory which is love beyond compare. 3. Those to whom good deeds are the supreme thought, they finally attain the abode of Brahma.. Those who perform sacrifices go to Indra's heaven. 4. Those who have confidence in ancestral worship will finally live and move in the abode of those ancestors. Whatever God men worship they finally reach His abode. 5. Those who worship the evil demons become like them after death. So those who give ear to the stories of the saints will finally attain Vaikuṇṭha (the Heaven of Vishṇu). 6. The moment Chakrapāṇi sees his *bhaktas* in distress He comes to drive it from them, and finally giving them his own four-armed form provides them a place in the home of full-union-with-God. 7. Such a promise Paṇḍhari has given in connection with this book. Therefore, O Hearers, listen with a reverent and loving heart.

8. At the close of the last chapter we saw how the Husband-of-Rukmiṇi revealed himself to Bhānudās, and how deciding to become free from all worldly desires, Bhānudās gave up his commercial affairs.

THE KING OF VIDYĀNAGARA HEARS OF THE GLORY OF VIṬHOBĀ.

9. Now listen to the following tale. There was a Brāhman living in the sacred city of Paṇḍhari. Feeling the desire in his heart for money he started on a country to country begging trip. 10. Visiting many towns and cities in his journey, he arrived finally at Vidyānagara. Entering the city, he thought to himself, "I must meet the king." 11. So the Brāhman took his bath, performed his devotions and then attempted to enter the palace. The doorkeeper would not let him go inside, however. He said

to him, "Just wait here a little while. 12. I will at once bring the king's permission; then, sir, you may enter within the palace." The servant returned from informing the king, and the Brāhman then entered within. 13. Rām Rājā, when he saw the Brāhman, bowed and worshipped him. The Brāhman felt exceeding joy, and exclaimed, "Blessed are you, O King, the very image of Charity." 14. The king then enquired, "From whence have you come, sir? With what desire in your heart have you come? Please tell me." 15. To this enquiry of the king the Brāhman replied with joy thus: "The sacred city of Paṇḍhari is a most wonderful city. It is there that I dwell. 16. I have heard of your generosity and have hastened here begging from country to country on my way." The king listened to his story and felt keen pleasure. 17. The king replied to the Brāhman, "Let your mind be at ease. I am going now first to my bath, and then to the worship of the Goddess. 18. Come with me and see her temple. The temple glitters with gold. I shall make to her the various offerings, and present her with the *tulsi* leaf." 19. The Brāhman was delighted with this conversation with the king, and accompanied him as he went to worship the Goddess. 20. The king had planted costly flower gardens around the temple. In the inner temple he had placed the image of Ambikā. Here he now performed the appropriate ceremonies of worship. 21. These were accompanied by the loud noise of many musical instruments. While the king performed his part of the worship, the Brāhmans repeated *mantras*. The loud noise was a joyful one. 22. In worshipping the Goddess they used the sixteen rites, they clothed Her with garments, and adorned Her with jewels. Thus adorned with these various divine jewels the Goddess looked beautiful. 23. They perfumed her with sandal oil and other scents. Around her neck was placed a garland of flowers. With incense and lights the king made his offerings. 24. Lighting the five lamps he waved them before Mahāmāyā, and fell at Her feet, making a prostrate *namaskār*. 25. After distributing gifts the king sat for a while in quiet contemplation. He then entered into conversation with the Brāhman from Paṇḍhari.

26. "You see," said he, "you may hunt throughout the three worlds, and yet you will not find a divinity the equal of Rājāi. I have never seen or heard of her equal. Blessed is Her boundless marvellousness! 27. You also see with your own eyes this beautiful temple. It is plated with silver. Around it I have planted this flower garden, that I may worship the Mother-of-the-World with flowers. 28. All the people of Vidyānagara come here to worship Her. I have commissioned my ministers to Her service. The special rites of Worship I perform myself. 29. You live at Paṇḍhari, but its glory cannot be equal to that here. It is hardly possible that Pāṇḍuraṅg can be worshipped with such pomp as Rājāi is worshipped here. 30. When it is poor Brāhmans who have to do the worshipping how can they provide such garments and adornments as those I provide." The Brāhman listened to these words of the king, and his heart became filled with anger.

THE BRĀHMAN EXTOLS THE GLORY OF VIṬHOBĀ OF PĀṆḌHARPUR.

31. "Kings of kings," said he, "you, in your vain pride, without even having seen Paṇḍhari, boast of your own divinity as alone great. 32. You have plated the temple with silver, and you proclaim to men that ornamentation. But our sacred city was built by Viśvakarmā, and plated

with gold. 33. There are forests there of the Wishing-tree. Touch-stones and wishing-stones lie about like common pebbles. Divine floating banners flash everywhere like lightning. 34. There are herds of wishing-cows there. The tulsi altars are set with jewels. And here loving Vaishṇavas joyfully perform kīrtans. 35. The river Chandrabhāgā is there flowing with nectar. She is the mistress of all sacred waters. By the mere sight of her men become freed from this worldly existence and attain Heaven. 36. The beautiful Rambhā and Tilottamā come and dance on the eagle-platform. Gandharvas sing by the door of the temple, and space itself overflows with their music. 37. The God-of-Gods, the Husband-of-Rukmiṇi, who was living blissfully in the Ocean-of-milk, when He saw his *bhakta* Puṇḍalik there, He came at once to that spot. 38. And Chakrapāṇi, placing his hands on his hips, has remained standing there. If he sees any of his *bhaktas* in distress, He immediately comes in person to their relief. 39. Lakshmi even becomes ashamed of Herself as Her eyes behold His glorious form. Ten millions of suns hide themselves away before the glory of His crown. 40. Fair of complexion, delicate in form, holding the bow, his yellow garment tucked tightly about him, his glorious bewitching face is adorned with the divine earrings of alligator shape. 41. In order to see this form of his with their own eyes, Indra, and the three hundred and thirty million gods, stand constantly before him with hands, palm to palm, and reverently and lovingly praise him. 42. He whose name the Dweller-in-Kailas repeats to himself day and night; He whom the Vedas and Śastras describe; He whose limits Brahmadeva even does not know; 43. He whom the Serpent praised with his thousand mouths, each tongue splitting into two, and then settled into queitude. 44. Such an one is the divinity Pāṇḍuraṅg. Such is the holy city of Paṇḍhari, Such is the purifying water of the Chandrabhāgā. Nowhere else are such to be seen in the three worlds. 45. Without first paying attention to all this, you vainly praise your own works of ornamentation. Rājāī is your family goddess, but I care nothing for her. 46. Why! She comes regularly to Paṇḍhari and there she performs the service of sweeping the temple and smearing it with cow-dung." As the Brāhman thus spoke the king became furious with rage.

THE ENRAGED KING THREATENS THE BRĀHMAN.

47. "Before my very face he has insulted the deity whom I worship," the king exclaimed. "Heedless of what he is doing, he sings the praise of his own deity. 48. I ought to put him to death, but being a ruler I would be blamed. So I will punish the Brāhman and drive him away to regions out of the city. 49. The king, therefore, said to the Brāhman, "You have spoken falsely. I certainly have never heard of this golden Pandharpur. 50. And this Goddess, Rājāī, who continually remains here where she first revealed herself, you, with your own mouth have called her a slave of Pāṇḍuraṅg. I am going to punish you, and drive you away into the jungle." 51. The Brāhman replied, "Hear, O king! I have told you the exact truth, You should come at once to Paṇḍhari, and see the Husband-of-Rukmiṇi for yourself. 52. His glory is ten million times as great as I have described it. If (after coming to Paṇḍhari) you do not see it to be so, then you may rightly punish me. 53. So long as you have not seen the God-of-Gods, this Rājāī seems to you to be great, just

as a lamp light seems bright only so long as the sun has not arisen. 54. So long as one has not seen the elephant of Indra, other elephants seem great . The stars seem bright only so long as the full moon has not arisen. 55. One praises other juices only so long as one has not obtained nectar. So long as one has not seen the ocean, a river seems extraordinarily great. 56. Until one has seen a forest of Wishing-trees, one delights in a mango grove. Until one has listened to the wisdom of the Vedanta, one is pleased with heretical doctrines. 57. So long as one has not seen the mountain of gold, so long it is brass that glitters. So until one has seen Paṇḍharināth one is satisfied with other deities," 58. The king listened and responded, "I will at once hasten to Paṇḍhari, and if I see there things just as you have described them to me, then only will it be well with you, O Twice-born. 59. But if you have told me untruths, then I shall immediately punish you." The king then commanded his ministers to prepare the equipment for the journey.

60. Accompanied by horses, elephants, chariots, palanquins, and a small army, the king started on his journey that he might see Pāṇḍuraṅg. 61. They marched along to the sound of many musical instruments. Behind them all, walked the Brāhman, thinking to himself, "The Husband-of-Rukmiṇi will, either protect me from humiliation in my need, or He will disregard me. 62. If the king does not see things as I have described them to him, he will undoubtedly punish me." 63. So bringing the image of Pāṇḍuraṅg to his mind, he praised him from his heart, and prayed, "O Thou, who tenderly carest for *bhaktas*, Husband-of-Rukmiṇi, come to my rescue in this hour of my need. 64. I, your Brāhman, helpless and poor, went on my country to country begging journey. Through the

proclaiming of Thy name I have gained support for my family. 65. O God, The saints of old have proclaimed Thy wondrous renown. And I have but described the same renown to the king, but he is unable to regard it as true. 66. The king has become angry at what he calls an insult to his family Goddess, and he is now on his way to witness for himself, O Pāndharināth. 67. I have related to the king what Paṇḍhari really is. It is only in this Kaliyuga that it seems to men to be built of earthen walls, for there is no essential difference (between gold and earth). 68. Just as coins buried by some ancestor appear to the luckless man as mere charcoal, so Pandhari, though really golden, seems otherwise through a wrong conception. 69. As the saints of old have described Paṇḍhari, in those same words I have described it. But now if the king does not see Chakrapāṇi as I have portrayed Him, he will punish me. 70. Then I shall commit suicide, and the words of the saints will be proved false. Moreover, when good people will hereafter read about the glory of Paṇḍhari, they will not believe it. 71. O protector of the helpless, Husband-of-Rukmiṇi, in this my present distres come quickly to my rescue.

This appeal of the Brāhman for mercy, made the Saviour-of-the-world aware of his need. 72. He thought to Himself, "Because the Brāhman has extolled my profound renown, he is being dishonoured, so I shall have to make things seem as he has described them." 73. And with this the Holder-of-the-Bow said to Rukmiṇi, "The king of Vidyānagara is hastening here on his way to see us. 74. Paṇḍhari in reality excels all that the city of Dvārakā was. We must show this to the king in the twinkling of an eye, and thus remove his doubts. 75. If we do not do this, the Brāhman will be punished. He will then take his own life.

Our reputation will suffer loss, and the saints and good people will laugh at us." 76. The Mother-of-the-World, after listening to these words, made at once a *namaskār* at His feet, and said, "I shall bring here at once the buildings of Heaven and show them to the king." 77. No sooner did she think this, than in less than a moment it all took place, and by so doing the Life-of-the-World, expert in the use of Māyā, magnified the glory of his *bhakta*.

THE KING HAS A GLORIOUS VISION.

78. Now let us turn to Rām Rājā as he was hastening along and arriving near Paṇḍharpur, and while the Brāhman in great fright was imploring the aid of the Husband-of-Rukmiṇi. 79. Rām Rājā called to the Brāhman into his presence and said, "If you do not now satisfy my doubts, I shall bring you to dishonour." 80. He called for an elephant to be brought to him, and seated himself on its canopied seat. (From this height) he gazed at the city of Pandhari and saw a strange and marvellous sight. 81. Just as the constellations appear about the full moon, so around about the pinnacle of the temple lustrous buildings seemed to glitter. 82. As the king saw this wonder he was overwhelmed with amazement, and exclaimed "Paṇḍhari looks exactly as the Brāhman has described it to me." 83. Repentant in heart, the king descended from the elephant, and making a prostrate *namaskār* to the Brāhman said, 84. "I see before me exactly what you described to me. It was my ignorance that made me proud, and led me to wrong thoughts. 85. With these words the king again made the Brāhman a *namaskār*, and freeing his mind of all ill feeling he sat at his feet. 86. The Brāhman himself was also amazed, and exclaimed, "The Husband-of-Rukmiṇi has indeed come to my rescue." The three-worlds could not

contain his joy, and with love he sang His praise. 87. "Chief among *bhaktas* and their head-jewel was Puṇḍalik," he sang, "and Chakrapāni came from Dvārakā to see him. 88. Of all the sacred waters the Ganges is considered the chief, and yet the Chandrabhāgā surpasses her. By the mere sight of her the world is purified. She permits no place for pride. 89. It is true that the Life-of-the-World dwells in such places as Mathurā, Gokul, and Vrindāvana. Śri Krishṇa resides also in Dvārakā for the sake of his *bhaktas*. 90. But to me the glory of this sacred place seems incomparable." Thus with utter abandonment the Brāhman in his love sang of the glories of Paṇḍhari. 91. The king now had cymbals and drums brought and made a celebration. He gathered together the Vaishṇava *bhaktas*, and loud was the joyful noise they made. 92. As the king continued gazing, he saw before him a forest of Wishing-trees, and touch-stones, and wishing-stones lying about like pebbles.

He approached the open lands around Paṇḍhari. 93. Here there were innumerable wishing-cows all round. The king amazed, ejaculated, "Blessed are these infinite wonders." 94. Holding the Brāhman's hand the king continued gazing. He saw the resplendent city of Paṇḍhari and his eyes were dazzled by it. 95. He saw various birds sitting on the trees, singing in their delight. Swans and peacocks danced, strutting about in their joy. 96. Ascetics were performing their austerities. Brāhmans were studying the Vedas. The *bhaktas* of Vishṇu with drum and viṇā were singing His praise. 97. Temple-women, collected here and there in groups, were dancing, thereby compelling eyes to stare at them, and infatuating sensually minded men. 98. Here and there saints were sitting discussing the supreme Soul, and as they experienced absorption into that Soul they embraced one another. 99. One hundred and eight sacred rivers, taking a bodily form, came and bathed in the Chandrabhāgā, and were purified, and this took place while the king was looking on. 100. A golden tulsi altar had been erected, studded with gems, and the tulsi adorned with garments and jewels was being worshipped by men and women. 101. The king having first bathed in the Bhīmarathi then went to see and worship the God, and, behold, Indra, and all the other gods were also there, beholding the Lord-of-Paṇḍhari. 102. All the eight supernatural Powers, as slaves, were personally serving about the God. Suddenly the king recognized Rājāī amongst them. 103. "She is our family Goddess whom we adore in our worship in Vidyānagara," he exclaimed, "and she is sweeping the dooryard here at Paṇḍhari!" The king was amazed. 104. "Udo!" the king called out to her, and began immediately to question her. "Mother," he asked, "why are you here? You are here sweeping with your own hands!" 105. Bhavāni replied, "You hold vain pride in your heart. Endless female slaves like myself come here to Paṇḍhari to serve. 106. Here to this dooryard of Puṇḍalik all sacred waters come, and prostrating themselves on the ground, thereby becoming immediately pure, let their waters flow." 107. Still amazed, the king looked further, and saw to his surprise Nārad ṛishi and Tumbara, singing the God's praise. 108. Males and females, with four arms, were seen as actual beings. The king threw himself prostrate before them, in the fulness of his joy. 109. Both the Gods, Victory and Conquest, holding weapons, such as the shell, disk, and others, stood before the temple door. Divine banners flashed like lightning in the heavens.

110. After prostrating himself on the ground the king entered the temple. As he saw the light from the God he

had to close his eyes, and hold on to the hand of the Brāhman. 111. Then there met his gaze the *saguṇ* form of the Fair-Complexioned, Delicate-one, Lotus-eyed Clothed-in-the-yellow-silk-robe, Lotus-eyed, Smiling-faced, Life-of-the-World. 112. That form which is the object of the Yogi's meditation; that form which the Five-faced contemplates in his heart; that form, which when one attempts to describe, all descriptions are seen to fall short of reality. 113. When describing the taste of nectar what other sweet juice is there with which it can be compared? So the God-of-Gods, the Husband-of-Rukmiṇi, though he can be seen, cannot be compared. 114. Those who are his *bhaktas* can see Him with their eyes. They alone, through actual experience, know the marks by which He is to be recognized. The mere wise, who undertake to praise Him, become as dumb as the Vedas. 115. The king then with love embraced the incomparable image of the Supreme Brahma. And gazing intently on His form, tightly clasped His feet. 116. The king now said to the Brāhman, "You are my dear friend, my *sadguru,* my close companion. How can I thank you enough for your kindness! You have enabled me to meet the Eagle-bannered-one. 117. I have here seen things ten million times as wonderful as you described them. I have seen the Lord-of-Heaven with my own eyes, and have felt its exceeding joy. 118. I also saw my family Goddess, Rājāī, sweeping the threshold of the temple, and Indra also, accompanied by other Gods, standing there with their hands palm to palm. 119. I now see nowhere in the three-worlds a city as wonderful as Paṇḍhari, a deity as supreme as Pandharināth, and a purifying stream like the Chandrabhāgā." 120. There was once an insect inside of a fig, who thought to itself, "This is my vast universe." When the fig was broken open and it looked round about, its mind was lost in wonder. 121. So it happened to the king, and clasping the Brāhman's feet he cried out, "I was enveloped by ignorance, but through you I have been freed from it." 122. But now suddenly all the marvellous vision which had been shown to the king vanished, and lo! his eyes now saw only the earthen walls, to his great astonishment. 123. The sacred city of Paṇḍhari is in reality what was shown to the king, but because of the effects of a man's *karma* it seems to him to be of earthen walls. 124. The king with amazed mind now saw the city just as it appears to us to-day, and he exclaimed, "I have seen a great miracle."

THE KING TAKES THE IMAGE OF VIṬHOBĀ TO VIDYĀNAGARA.

125. The king now thought to himself, "Why should I now in vain worship Bhavāni? If the Ocean-of-Milk is near at hand, why should I leave it to bathe in river water. 126. If I see a lake of nectar, why should I take even heaven-made medicines? When a wishing-tree is close by, one should not sit in the shade of a bābul tree. 127. Why throw away the touchstone already in one's hand, and become an alchemist. If a wishing-cow comes to one's house, why worship a goat? 128. When the sun is shining into the house, why bring in a lamp? So having had a vision of Pāṇḍuraṅg, why now worship a Goddess? 129. Thus reasoning with himself Rām Rājā besought the Eagle-bannered-One thus, "God-of-Gods, King-of-Heaven, fulfil the desire of my heart. 130. I have the desire in my heart to take you to Vidyānagara. So giving to me, your suppliant, the assurance of your blessing, come along quickly with me, O God, my king." 131. The God re-

plied "(I agree to come) but if you, during the journey, should rest me on the ground, I shall certainly remain at that very spot. Or if in your kingdom you are guilty of any injustice, I shall come back to Paṇḍhari." 132. As Chakrapāṇi thus replied, the king was overjoyed in heart. "I shall place relays of men at intervals along the route, and thus take the God with me," he said to himself. 133. And with this idea he stationed men in the interval from the sacred city of Paṇḍhari as far as Vidyānagara, and taking the idol (out of the temple) started to carry it away. 134. The officiating Brāhmans did not resist. They knew their power could not prevail against that of the king. The idol was lifted up and carried along from hand to hand. 135. Thus Pāṇḍuraṅg was carried along swiftly to Vidyānagara, and there installed. The king, in his own person, performed the installation rites, and the ceremonies of worship.

PAṆḌHARPUR WITHOUT VIṬHOBĀ.

136. Now let us turn to Paṇḍharpur, where in the month of Ashāḍh, Vaishṇavas arrived on their pilgrimage. Here they learned the fact that the God had gone to Vidyānagara. 137. Paṇḍharpur now seemed desolate, like a body without life, or like a river without water. The city was oppressed with fears. 138. It was like an army without a king, like constellations without the moon, or as a virtuous, devoted wife, deprived of her husband, seems unprotected among men. 139. So with Hari gone to Vidyānagara, the whole of Paṇḍhari seemed desolate. Dejected, the saints and *mahants* sat down by the Eagle-platform. 140. "Whose praises can we now sing," they said among themselves. "The Life-of-the-World has deserted us. The promise he gave to Puṇḍalik (to remain

here always) has become a broken promise." 141. Pious *bhaktas* arrived and all exclaimed, "What has happened to the King-of-Paṇḍhari? And all learned the news that the God had gone to Vidyānagara. 142. The saints, sadhus, and other Vaishṇavas said to one another, "Some one should go to Vidyānagara and bring back the Husband-of-Rukmiṇi." 143. They discussed this proposal among themselves, but no one gave any assurance that he would go on such an errand. Some indeed remarked, "Pāṇḍurang has paid no regard to his promise to Puṇḍalik. He will not come back by any effort of ours." 144. Another added, "We have no entrée into the king's palace. If the king should learn the purpose of our coming he would punish us well." 145. One brought forward an excuse from the point of view of the attributelessness of God. "God is within us," he argued. "If we have no experience of this the philosophers (knowers of self) will have misled us." 146. Still another added, "Whatever and however anything takes place it is by the will of God. We should watch it, but let no one be troubled thereby."

BHĀNUDĀS OFFERS TO GO AND BRING VIṬHOBĀ BACK.

147. In this group of saints was Bhānudās, the Vaishṇava *bhakta*. He gave them a solemn assurance, saying, "I will go, and bring back the Husband-of-Rukmiṇi, or give up my life in the attempt." 148. And with these words he started at once. Arriving at Vidyānagara at night time he began to question the people. 149. "The king has brought here, from Paṇḍhari the image of Pāṇḍurang. Tell me quickly where he has installed it." 150. From fear of the king no one was willing to tell him

the facts, and would reply, "We do not know." 151. Bhānudās then asked some one privately, and was told by a Vaishṇava *bhakta* that the king had installed the God in the palace temple, and that he worshipped him in private; 152. That after the king had worshipped him no one was allowed to see Him; that the king had put padlocks on the doors of the temple, and stationed a guard for His protection. 153. When Bhānudās heard this he became full of joy. Midnight arrived, and all of the guard were asleep. 154. When Bhānudās approached the door of the temple, at that moment the padlock dropped. He entered within and prostrated himself before the God. 155. He gazed for a moment on the God's form, and then lovingly embraced Him. With a voice, choked with emotion, he thus pled with Him.

BHĀNUDĀS CHIDES THE GOD AND PLEADS.

156. "Husband-of-Rukmiṇi, Dweller-in-Vaikuṇṭhā, Giver-of-the promise to Puṇḍalik, King-of-the-Yādavas, have you dropped your affection for us and become subject to the king? 157. You gave a promise to Puṇḍalik that you would never go away from Paṇḍhari. And now this promise is seen to be false. 158. It is evident you do not care for our lowly worship. The king here worships you with the sixteen rites. Regarding that as happiness, you, Vishṇu, Eagle-bannered-One, choose to remain here. 159. Because of these heavenly garments, and adornments, and his offerings of various dainty foods you have lost recollection of us, poor people! 160. O Purushottama, you have left Rukmiṇi, Rādhā, and Satyabhāmā. O Dark-as-a-Cloud, the king by his professions of love has caused you to leave us. 161. You have left Paṇḍharpur and made

Vidyānagara your abode. But great *ṛishis* and noble *bhaktas* are waiting there for you. 162. Rambhā, Tillottmā, Urvaśi, Meṇakā, and the eight leaders of song came there to serve you, but leaving them, O Father-of-Brahmadeva, you have comfortably settled yourself here! 163. Or is it because of some awful fault of ours, the fear of which has caused you to run away from us? Or may it be because we have asked of you tokens of your love, that you have run away? 164. Can it be that it is the noise and confusion in the *kīrtans,* whereby you are unable to sleep? And so you have selected for yourself this quiet spot. I now understand what the facts are. 165. Or could it be the countless pilgrims who gather there, in meeting whom you become weary, that has made you to come here to Vidyānagara for a quiet rest?" 166. The Life-of-the-World listened to these chidings of Bhānudās, and replied, "You are speaking without due thought these disconsolate words. 167. I am not enjoying these many kinds of rites with which I am worshipped, nor these garments, adornments, and ornaments. My soul is really pining away for a sight of the banks of the Bhimā river. 168. It is the king who has brought me here and imprisoned me. And you have also hardened your hearts, in that no one has come here to take me back. 169. I used to give you prosperity, supernatural powers, and the four forms of Deliverance, but you used to worship me out of love alone, disregarding those benefits. 170. Aside from those benefits I had nothing I could give you. So that my debt to you, incurred by your service of love, I was unable to repay, hence I deserted you." 171. As the Husband-of-Rukmiṇi uttered these words (of explanation), he became choked with emotion. But tears of joy flowed from his eyes, and moved by mutual love both sobbed together. 172. The

Life-of-the-World then embraced Bhānudās, and said, "Tomorrow in the early morning, as you worship, I shall reveal myself to you." 173. The Holder-of-the-Bow then removed his necklace of nine jewels and placed it on Bhānudās, adding, "Hasten now to your lodgings, for the king will soon be coming to worship me." 174. As soon as Bhānudās had stepped outside, the padlock returned again to its place on the door. Thus the God had met his *bhakta* without any one having the least knowledge of it.

175. The king arose early, performed immediately his bath, and lovingly bowing to the God, waved before him the burning wick-lights. 176. Suddenly he missed the string of jewels on the God's neck. The king enquired at once of the officiating priests. "What thief has been here?" he demanded, and he flew into a rage. 177. He gave them a severe beating and cried out, "Bring back at once the string of jewels. If you cannot produce those priceless jewels you must search for them the whole world over." 178. No sooner was this order given, than a house to house search was made, but nowhere could the string of jewels be found. Then they began to look for thieves outside the city. 179. And lo! there sat Bhānudās on the bank of the Gaṅgā river. He had had his bath and was repeating the names of God. The king's officers looked attentively at him, and spied from afar the string of jewels on his neck. 180. "We have found the thief," they shouted. "Let us seize him." The king's servants at once bound the noble Vaishṇava, and carried him along. 181. As he was brought into the city every one laughed as they saw him, and mocking him said, "This fellow is wandering about in the guise of a saint, in order to deceive the people. 182. Look! He has placed violent hands on a God. Is he

likely to nave any fear of man? If a butcher met even the cow, Kapilā, would he so much as think of worshipping her?"

183. Thus many kinds and classes of men derided Bhānudās as they saw him being carried along. But Bhānudā showed no sign of being troubled thereby, and continued repeating the names of God. 184. One observer reminded the crowd of a proverb, "A garland of the sacred tulsi around the neck of a high-way robber," adding "Our eyes have seen the truth of this proverb to-day. This man is evidently the one who stole the string of jewels." 185. The officers now took the string of nine jewels and brought them to the king, exclaiming, "We have bound the thief, and brought him to you. Who is to punish him?" 186. In a great rage the king cried out, "Impale him at once!" But in so ordering, he did it without taking thought that he ought to find out who the man was, and what kind of a thief he was. 187. Bhānudās said to the officers, "My death is at hand. Allow me, therefore, in these my last moments to see and worship Pāṇḍuraṅg." 188. There were some good men among these officers, and they paid respect to Bhānudās' request. Obtaining the king's permission they took Bhānudās to the temple. 189. Bhānudās said to the God, "Evidently it is because I came to take you away secretly that you have devised this plan to have me punished by the king. So be it! 190. Deprive of life whoever comes here to take you away, and enjoying wanton pleasures in this palace of the king, remain happily here! 191. Was it with this thought in mind, O Dark-complexioned-one, that you put the string of jewels around my neck? And yet as you talked with me tears flowed from your eyes. 192. Be it so, and yet to the end of my hundred

thousand births I will never leave you, O Husband-of-Rukmiṇi." And with these words he lovingly made an obeisance to the God. 193. The officers now cried, "Get up! Hustle! If to begin with, you had not commi. this theft nothing of this kind would have taken place." 194. With these words the officers dragged Bhānudās outside the temple. They placed the impaling stake on his shoulder, and applied *śendur* to his forehead. 195. Numberless men and women assembled to see the unusual spectacle. They led Bhānudās outside the city, and hastened to fasten the sharp stake in the ground. 196. As they were about to lift him up onto it, to impale him, Bhānudās thus supplicated God, "Let the very heavens fall crashing upon me, yet will I remember Thee. 197. Though the seven oceans should unite, and overwhelm me, still I will not leave Thee, God, my king. I wave as an offering before Thee this destructible body of mine. 198. Though the whole earth should go to destruction, and the five elements be dissolved, yet aside from Thee, O Husband-of-Rukmiṇi, I need no one at my side. 199. When the submarine fire shall devour the Three Worlds, thou wilt be my beloved still." The Life-of-the-World, seeing the determination of Bhānudās, came to his rescue. 200. A most wonderful, a most strange marvel, now took place. Listen ye *bhaktas* with reverence to what now happened. The impaling stake, fastened in the ground, suddenly burst into leaf. 201. It blossomed into flower and fruit. The officers of the king went and told him what had taken place, adding, "He is a Vaishṇava *bhakta.* Pāṇḍuraṅg has come to his rescue. 202. The impaling stake has turned into a green tree." The king listened to the story told by his servants, of what had taken place, and expressed his great astonishment. 203. He hastened to the scene, and saw the tree with his own eyes.

Remorse now seized his heart, and he cried out, "I have committed a great wrong." 204. The king then made Bhānudās an obeisance in love and reverence, and said, "From lack of thought I have done you this wrong."

205. Without delaying, the king took Bhānudās to the temple. And when the image of Pāṇḍuraṅg saw them, it became choked with emotion. 206. As Bhānudās embraced its feet, the Life-of-the-World raised him up and embraced him. The Husband-of-Rukmiṇi said to Bhānudās, "You have suffered much because of me. 207. Take me up now on your shoulder and carry me to Paṇḍharpur. There at the door of Puṇḍalik's shrine I will dwell forever." 208. The king now clasped the feet of the God, and cried, "Are you leaving me, with no concern for me." The God replied, "You have committed a wrong, though unintentionally, it is true. 209. You have performed some good deeds, and therefore I have remained here with you for these many days. But I must go now. Henceforth keep my form in remembrance in your heart with love." 210. Bhānudās now said to the Husband-of-Rukmiṇi, "How am I able to lift and carry you? Moreover I have not the kingly power to collect many men to bear you." 211. The-Merciful-to-the-Humble replied, "I am entirely at your service. All my powers are now yours, my *bhakta*." 212. With this the Life-of-the-World assumed a diminutive form, and said to Bhānudās, "Put me in your deer-skin bag, and take me along." 213. Bhānudās went at once for his bag and placed Chakrapāṇi inside.

Now, let no one who hears this story have doubts about it. 214. For example, space is of infinite expanse, yet as you look into a jar, the space there is only as large as the jar. So the God in love, to please his *bhakta* became small in size. 215. Or again, there are many great currents of air, but if one uses a fan, one makes a current of air of the same nature as the others. So the Husband-of-Rukmiṇi, of his own free will, became subject to his *bhakta*. 216. Back in the time when Kṛishṇa was an avatar, as Yashodā was churning, her hand grasped him in the vessel, the same who now entered the little bag of Bhānudās. Why then should one doubt this story? 217. To one who looks with the eye of knowledge infinite space pervades a jar, and it looks the same as itself, whether in great or small sections, even if more minute than an atom. 218. So the Lord-of-the-World, out of affection for Bhānudās, fitted himself to the space of the deer-skin bag; and Bhāṇudās carrying it on his shoulder hastened on his return journey. 219. From out of this bag the Life-of-the-World spoke sweet words to his *bhakta*. "Blessed is this day, for in it we shall meet the saints and the other good people."

220. When Bhānudās arrived at the Lotus-lake he placed the Life-of-the-World on the ground, and with joy in his heart began his bath. 221. Suddenly the Husband-of-Rukmiṇi in the skin-bag became great in size, tearing to pieces the upper part where his head was, and the lower part (where his feet were). 222. When Bhānudās returned (from his bath) and saw what had happened he exclaimed, "God of Gods! What is this that you have done! You have become big again. How shall I now be able to lift you?" 223. The Husband-of-Rukmiṇi replied, "Go on at once and inform the saints and *sādhus*. They will come to welcome me back with loud music of many instruments. 224. And let them place me on my throne in an auspicious hour this

very day." In accordance with these words of Chakrapāṇi, Bhānudās started on his way.

225. Now by the Eagle-platform all the Vaishṇava *bhaktas* were sitting, oppressed with concern. "Bhānudās has been gone for many days," they exclaimed, "but the Husband-of-Rukmiṇi has not come back." 226. Just then suddenly they saw coming, the victorious *bhakta*, with his smiling face, calling out, "I have brought back the Recliner-on-the-Serpent." 227. Bhānudās embraced the saints, and said to them, "The Husband-of-Rukmiṇi has come as far as the Lotus-lake." Hearing this joyful news all were delighted. 228. Then with banners and flags the noble Vaishṇavas went out to welcome back the God, accompanied by the music of countless cymbals and drums. 229. Priests, rulers, men and women, joined the procession to welcome the God back. Arriving at the Lotus-lake they beheld the Dark-complexioned-one. 230. All prostrated themselves on the ground, and then after embracing the God they put him, the Husband-of-Rukmiṇi, on a chariot and carried him along in an enthusiastic procession. 231. The saints loudly proclaimed his praise. Dancers danced wildly before him. Drums and other musical instruments sounded aloud, and all felt joy. 232. In describing that occasion there are no comparisons that are sufficient, and yet in that month of Kārtik the pilgrims saw that sight with their own eyes. 233. When at full moon a chariot procession takes place, that procession is the nearest comparison that can be made. It was then thus that Pāṇdharināth passed along in pompous procession. 234. When the procession arrived at the bank of the Chandrabhāgā, the leaders among them came forward, bathed the God, and then all started on their way to the great door of the

temple. 235. They took the dark coloured idol from off the chariot and passing it from hand to hand, placed it in a palanquin. They carried it along to the temple and there anointed it with the special ceremonies for a welcome back. 236. Brāhmans repeated *mantras* aloud. Vaishṇavas sang lustily His Praises. The Pervader-of-the-universe sat now on His throne, Blessed was this happy day! 237 With garments, ornaments, adornments, and the sixteen rites they worshipped Him. Offering Him dainty food, and other offerings, they invoked His blessing. 238. Priests made offerings to the God of handfuls of flowers, with loud repetitions of *mantras*. Saints, Vaishṇavas, and the pilgrims, all felt the joy of the occasion.

239. And now the assembled crowd of men and women praised Bhānudās saying that it was through Him that the Lord-of-Heaven had come back to Paṇḍhari. 240. Some distributed sweetmeats throughout the city. Others gave feasts of daintily cooked food to Brāhmans. Thus all the dwellers of that sacred city rejoiced in heart. 241. Just as, when the son of Rāghu came back to Ayodhyā, after enduring fourteen years of exile, the people of the city rejoiced, so the people rejoiced in the same way. 242. As when a mountain becomes dry in a time of drought, and then a cloud pours abundant rain upon it, (as it rejoices) so the people of Paṇḍhari rejoiced. 243. It was as when the clouds rejoiced when they saw the ocean issuing from the Ṛishi Agasti. 244. It was as when the Spring comes and all vegetation appears beautiful. So was it at the return of the Protector-of-the-Helpless to Paṇḍhari. All the inhabitants were happy. 245. It was as when life returns to the body and all the senses are quickened and begin to perform their functions. So it happened to all the people of Paṇḍhari.

246. As one listens to the interesting story in the next chapter he will gain faultless victory. Therefore, O *bhaktas,* peacefully gain it for yourselves. 247. As the glorious Husband-of-Rukmiṇi increases the glory of His good saints, so His slave, Mahipati, sings of their noble characters. 248. Swasti. The Lord-of-the-World will be satisfied as he listens to this book, the Bhaktavijaya. This is the delightful forty-third chapter. Chapter 43rd, verses 248.

Appendix I

परिशिष्ट १.

महिपतिकृत भक्तविजय

अध्याय ४२वा.

श्रीगणेशाय नमः ॥ श्रीकृष्णाय नमः ॥ ॥ जय जय वासुदेवा जगन्नाथा ॥ कमललोचना रुक्मिणीकांता ॥ निजभक्तांसी सुखदाता ॥ तुजविण सर्वथा असेना ॥ १ ॥ जय जय पद्मनाभा विश्वमूर्ति ॥ विधिजनका वैकुंठपति ॥ विराट्स्वरूपा वामनमूर्ति ॥ अगम्यस्थिति वेदशास्त्रां ॥ २ ॥ जय विश्वबाहो अपरिमिता ॥ विश्वचक्षु तूं देखता ॥ विश्वपदीं गमनकर्ता ॥ निगम वार्ता बोलतसे ॥ ३ ॥ हे विराट्स्वरूपा हृषीकेशी ॥ सर्वथा न कळेच निजभक्तांसी ॥ मग सगुणस्वरूप धरून तयांसी ॥ आपुले भजनासी लाविलें ॥ ४ ॥ ते जैसी इच्छा धरिती चित्तीं ॥ तैसाच होसी क्षीराब्धिजापती ॥ जैसें बाळकासी धरून हातीं ॥ चाले हंसगती निजमाता ॥ ५ ॥ तें बोबडें बोले मंजुळ वचन ॥ तेणेंच संतोषे तिचें मन ॥ मग तैसेंच आपणही बोलून ॥ देत चुंबन निजप्रीतीं ॥ ६ ॥ तेवीं भक्तांसी कांहीं न कळतां ज्ञान ॥ आणि वेडेंवाकुडें करितां स्तवन ॥ तूं तैसाचि होसी जगज्जीवन ॥ निजकृपेनें आपुल्या ॥ ७ ॥ मागिले अध्यायीं अनुसंधान ॥ मृत्युंजयचरित्र रसाळ गहन ॥ ऐकोनि श्रोते जाहले तल्लीन ॥ अगाध महिमान संतांचें ॥ ८ ॥ आतां साक्षात अवतार वासरमणी ॥ जाहला असे प्रतिष्ठानीं ॥ तें चरित्र रसाळ श्रवणीं ॥ परिसावें सज्जनीं निजप्रेमें ॥ ९ ॥ सूर्यउपासक एक ब्राह्मण ॥ सज्ञान पवित्र भाविक जाण ॥ तयासि जाहलें पुत्रनिधान ॥ संतोष मनीं वाटला ॥ १० ॥ तो दिवसेंदिवस जाहला थोर ॥ मग व्रतबंध केला सत्वर ॥ मायबापें तयावर ॥ लोभ अपार करिताती ॥ ११ ॥ अध्ययन

सांगतां त्याजकारण ॥ पिता जाहला क्रोधायमान ॥ मग तो त्या भयेंकरून ॥ गेला रुसोन पुत्र त्याचा ॥ १२ ॥ बाहेर जाऊनि करी तळमळ ॥ परी कोठें लपावया न मिळे स्थळ ॥ तंव अकस्मात एक देऊळ ॥ देखिलें तत्काळ दृष्टीसी ॥ १३ ॥ तें मेदिनींत गुप्त होतें जाण ॥ तेथें नाहीं मनुष्याचें आगमन ॥ मग सत्वर आंत प्रवेशोन ॥ बैसला लपोन त्या ठायीं ॥ १४ ॥ सूर्यनारायणाची मूर्ती ॥ त्या देवालयांत पुरातन होती ॥ त्याचे चरणीं सत्वरगती ॥ दंडवत प्रीतीं घातलें ॥ १५ ॥ मुलाचा भावार्थ देखोनी ॥ प्रसन्न जाहला वासरमणी ॥ म्हणे अज्ञान लेंकरूं असोन ॥ निश्चय मनीं धरिलासे ॥ १६ ॥ मग मनुष्यरूप धरूनि सत्वर ॥ तयासी भेटले दिवाकर ॥ दुग्ध पाजोनि पोटभर ॥ अभयवर दिधला ॥ १७ ॥ म्हणे निर्भय असों देईं मन ॥ श्रीपांडुरंगाचें करीं स्मरण ॥ कांहीं संकट पडतां जाण ॥ तुज मी पावेन तत्काळ ॥ १८ ॥ इकडे मायबापें उद्विग्न मानसीं ॥ धुंडिती निजपुत्रासी ॥ सप्त दिवस लोटतां त्यासी ॥ परी कोठें दृष्टीस पडेना ॥ १९ ॥ तंव एके दिवसीं ब्राह्मणकुमार ॥ अकस्मात आला बाहेर ॥ तेथें एक होता द्विजवर ॥ तेणें दृष्टीस देखिला ॥ २० ॥ हाक मारितांचि त्वरित ॥ तंव तो पळाला देवळांत ॥ ब्राह्मणें येऊनि नगरांत ॥ पित्यासी वृत्तांत सांगितला ॥ २१ ॥ पुत्राची शुद्धि लागतां देख ॥ मायबापांसी वाटला हरिख ॥ सवें घेऊनि ग्रामवासी लोक ॥ पाहावयासी चालिले ॥ २२ ॥ तों ओसाड देऊळ अरण्यांत ॥ देखोनि नवल करिती समस्त ॥ दिवट्या लाऊनियां त्वरित ॥ धीटपणें आंत उतरले ॥ २३ ॥ तंव नारायणाची मूर्ति नयनीं ॥ देखोनि तेथें सकळिकांनीं ॥ ब्राह्मणकुमार त्याचे चरणीं ॥ मस्तक ठेवून निजेला ॥ २४ ॥ मायबापें येऊनि जवळी ॥ पुत्रासी धरिलें हृदयकमळीं ॥ म्हणती एकटा कैसा वांचलास ये स्थळीं ॥ अश्रुपात डोळां लोटले ॥ २५ ॥ लोक पुसती त्याकारण ॥ तुझे कैसे वांचले प्राण ॥ क्षुधा तृषा लागतां जाण ॥ न मिळेचि अन्न या

ठायीं ॥ २६ ॥ म्हणे परम तेजस्वी देदीप्यमान ॥ येथें एक प्रकटला ब्राह्मण ॥ तो मज करवितो दुग्धपान ॥ तेणें प्राण वांचविले ॥ २७ ॥ ऐकूनि बालकाचें वचन ॥ आश्चर्य करिती सकळ जन ॥ म्हणती यासी भेटला सूर्यनारायण ॥ भावार्थ देखोन निजनिष्ठा ॥ २८ ॥ भास्कर प्रसन्न झाला त्यास ॥ म्हणोनि नाम ठेविलें भानुदास ॥ मग कडेवरी घेऊनि तयास ॥ आले नगरास आपुल्या ॥ २९ ॥ म्हणती ईश्वरें वांचविले याचे प्राण ॥ आतां न बोलावें कठिण वचन ॥ नारायणें आपुल्यासी पुत्रदान ॥ कृपा करून दिधलें ॥ ३० ॥ जैसी प्राक्तनीं असेल गती ॥ तैसेंच घडोन येईल पुढती ॥ आपण याची हळहळ चित्तीं ॥ व्यर्थ कासया करावी ॥ ३१ ॥ समाधान मानोनि चित्तीं ॥ मायबापांनीं धरिली प्रीती ॥ विद्याभ्यास सांगवा पुढती ॥ तरी जाईल मागुती रुसोनि ॥ ३२ ॥ वधू सत्वर विचारूनि जाण ॥ भानुदासाचें केलें लग्न ॥ ऐसे लोटतां बहुत दिन ॥ करित भजन श्रीहरीचें ॥ ३३ ॥ आयुष्य सरोनी गेलियावरी ॥ मायबापें निवर्तलीं ते अवसरीं ॥ परी भानुदास निर्भय अंतरीं ॥ प्रपंचव्यवहारीं गुंतेना ॥ ३४ ॥ न करी कवणाचें उपार्जन ॥ उदीम व्यवसाय घेणें देण ॥ न करी कदा राज-सेवन ॥ पांडुरंगभजन करीतसे ॥ ३५ ॥ घरीं पाहिजे वस्त्र अन्न ॥ कांतेचें हळहळीत मन ॥ मुलेंलेंकरें सर्व असोन ॥ उदास मन सर्वदा ॥ ३६ ॥ गृहस्थ मिळोनि चवघे जण ॥ भानुदासासी बोलती वचन ॥ कुटुंबासी पाहिजे वस्त्र अन्न ॥ तुम्हांकारण कळेना ॥ ३७ ॥ माता पिता होतीं शिरीं ॥ त्यांणीं संसार केला आजवरी ॥ पुढें कैसी होईल परी ॥ तुम्ही अंतरीं उदास ॥ ३८ ॥ विद्याभ्यासही फार ॥ तुम्हांसी नाहीं जी साचार ॥ आतां कांहीं सांगतों विचार ॥ तो परिसा सादर निजकर्णीं ॥ ३९ ॥ एकशत द्रव्य भांडवल जाण ॥ आम्ही देतसों तुम्हांकारण ॥ त्याचें कापड घेऊन ॥ चाटेपण करावें ॥ ४० ॥ नफा मिळेल तेणेंकरून ॥ कुटुंबासी करावें वस्त्र अन्न ॥ आमुचें मुद्दल जतन

करून ॥ हळूच देणें स्वइच्छा ॥ ४१ ॥ मग गृहस्थ जाऊनि बाजारासी ॥ कापड घेऊन दिधलें तयासी ॥ इतर उदीम होते त्यांसी ॥ भानुदासासी निरविलें ॥ ४२ ॥ म्हणती तुम्ही जातसां बाजारीं ॥ तेव्हां न्यावें यास बरोबरी ॥ बैसवूनि आपुले शेजारीं ॥ प्रपंचव्यवहारीं लावावें ॥ ४३ ॥ गृहस्थांचें वचन ऐकोनि कानीं ॥ मान्य केलें व्यवसायांनीं ॥ मग भानुदासासी सवें घेऊनी ॥ आपुले सन्निध बसविती ॥ ४४ ॥ मुळु उदानु अंगोळु ऐसी ॥ नंदभाषा सांगितली त्यासी ॥ केवला काठी पवित्रू त्यासी ॥ सांगोनियां दिधलें ॥ ४५ ॥ सेळू पोकू आणि ढकार ॥ आवारू खूण सांगती सत्वर ॥ कोणतें कैसें द्यावें अंबर ॥ हाही विचार सांगितला ॥ ४६ ॥ मुद्दल जतन करूनि जाण ॥ लाभ सांगावा विचारून ॥ कोणासी बोलतां सत्य वचन ॥ तरी होतसे हान निश्चितीं ॥ ४७ ॥ भानुदास बोले तयांप्रती ॥ मी असत्य न वदें कल्पांतीं ॥ कांहीं न मिळो मजप्रती ॥ परी सत्य निश्चितीं बोलेन ॥ ४८ ॥ व्यवसायी हांसती सकळिक ॥ म्हणती याचे कपाळीं लिहिली भीक ॥ म्हणोनि आमुचें नायके एक ॥ दरिद्री देख या नांव ॥ ४९ ॥ एक म्हणती लागलिया लांचे ॥ मग असत्य उदंड बोलेल वाचे ॥ प्रपंचव्यवहारीं बोलतां साचें ॥ कोणी दैवाचें दिसेना ॥ ५० ॥ जेवीं गर्भांधाचे दृष्टीस जाण ॥ अवघे आंधळे वाटती जन ॥ कीं रोग असतां शरीराकारण ॥ कडुवट पक्वान्न त्या भासे ॥ ५१ ॥ तेवीं आपुले अंतरीं असत्य नर ॥ तयासी न दिसे कोणी खरें ॥ जैसें जयाचें असेल अंतर ॥ तैसेच इतर भासती ॥ ५२ ॥ भानुदासाचें धैर्य मोठें ॥ प्रपंचव्यवहारीं न बोले खोटें ॥ सकळ लोकांसीं नवल वाटे ॥ देखोनि निकटें तयासी ॥ ५३ ॥ कोणी गिराईक पुरे अंबर ॥ त्यासी किंमत सांगे खरोखर ॥ इतका नफा मुदलावर ॥ एकद उत्तर बोलतसे ॥ ५४ ॥ चित्तास येईल तरी घेणं ॥ नाहीं तरी दुसरे दुकानीं जाणं ॥ इतुकें मात्र बोलोनि वचन ॥ मग नामस्मरण करीतसे ॥ ५५ ॥ जनीं जनार्दन

भरला जाण ॥ निश्चय कळला सगळांकारण ॥ म्हणती भानुदास असत्य वचन ॥ न बोलेचि कल्पांतीं ॥ ५६ ॥ ऐसें जाणोनि ग्राहिक ॥ त्यापासीं जाती सकळिक ॥ इतर व्यवसायी अकर्मिक ॥ दुरून कौतुक पाहाती ॥ ५७ ॥ म्हणती आपुल्या सवें लाविलें यासी ॥ तें बाधक जाहलें आपुल्यासी ॥ मग द्वेष उपजला मनासीं दुराचारियांसी तेधवां ॥ ५८ ॥ म्हणती आम्हां शेजारीं बैसतो ॥ आणि ग्राहिक आपणाकडे नेतो ॥ आम्ही तोंडाकडे टकमकां पाहतों ॥ पोटीं जळतों उगेचि ॥ ५९ ॥ एक म्हणती घालितो मोहनी ॥ तेणेंचि जन जाती भुलोनी ॥ मागितलें मोल देती टाकोनी ॥ घसघस कोणी करीना ॥ ६० ॥ एक म्हणती बैसला विश्वास ॥ तेणेंचि जन भजती त्यास ॥ आपण असत्य प्रपंचदास ॥ हें ईश्वरास मानेना ॥ ६१ ॥ एक म्हणती आतां बोलावें खरें ॥ दुजा देतसे प्रतिउत्तर ॥ आपुला विश्वास कोणी इतर ॥ यथार्थ साचार न मानिती ॥ ६२ ॥ एकदां वृत्ति टसावे जैसी ॥ तेचि जन्मवर चाले तैसी ॥ प्रत्यक्ष आपुल्या दृष्टीसी ॥ भानुदासासी घडली कीं ॥ ६३ ॥ श्वान उगेंच बैसलें घरीं ॥ आणि मनुष्यें चोरून नेल्या भाकरी ॥ तरी आळ येईल श्वानावरी ॥ कोणासी अंतरीं कळेना ॥ ६४ ॥ व्याघ्रें धरितां निजशांतीसी ॥ म्हणतील जपतो मारावयासी ॥ धन-लोभी होतांचि उदासी ॥ म्हणती नाडावयासी निघाला ॥ ६५ ॥ कीं जार तीर्थीं हिंडतां खरा ॥ म्हणती हा धुंडितो परदारा ॥ शांति धरूनि बैसतां मार्जारा ॥ म्हणती उंदिरा पाहतसे ॥ ६६ ॥ तेवीं आपुला जन्म असत्य बोलतां ॥ गेला असे सकळांदेखतां ॥ आतां यथार्थ जरी वर्ततां ॥ म्हणतील वृथा कपट हें ॥ ६७ ॥ आपुल्यादेखतां भानुदासाचा ॥ व्यवहार किंचित कापडाचा ॥ आतां तो थोर भाग्याचा ॥ ईश्वर तयाचा साहकारी ॥ ६८ ॥ आपण उदंड करितां भरोवरी ॥ परी पोटभर न मिळे भाकरी ॥ ऋणकरी येऊन बैसती द्वारीं ॥ आतां कैसी परी करावी ॥ ६९ ॥ भानुदासासी संगतीस लाविलें ॥ तैंपासोनि आपुलें

निघालें दिवाळें ॥ ग्राहिक त्याणें सकळ नेलें ॥ आम्ही तळमळ करीतसों ॥ ७० ॥ एके दिवसीं सकळ व्यवसायी ॥ बाजारासी गेले पाहीं ॥ वाट ओसरतां लवलाहीं ॥ देवळीं येऊन राहिले ॥ ७१ ॥ त्यांसवें भानुदास वैष्णवभक्त ॥ आले होते बाजारांत ॥ त्यांजशेजारीं बिऱ्हाड त्वरित ॥ त्याणें आणोनि लाविलें ॥ ७२ ॥ तंव त्या गांवांत हरिदास येऊन ॥ त्याणें रात्रीं मांडिलें कीर्तन ॥ गांवांत फिरतसे बोलावणें ॥ कथेसी येणें ह्मणोनि ॥ ७३ ॥ भानुदास ऐकोनि मात ऐसी ॥ उल्हास वाटला चित्तासी ॥ ह्मणे आज सुदिन एकादशी ॥ जावें कीर्तन ऐकावया ॥ ७४ ॥ व्यवसायियांसी ह्मणे ते अवसरीं ॥ आतां कीर्तनासी चलावें सत्वरीं ॥ आळस आणूनि न याल जरी ॥ निजाल बिऱ्हाडीं सकळिक ॥ ७५ ॥ तरी माझें दुकान रक्षून ॥ तुह्मी आपल्यापासीं करा जतन ॥ ऐकोनि भानुदासाचें वचन ॥ सक्रोधमन ते जाहले ॥ ७६ ॥ ह्मणती तूं जाहालासी देवलसी ॥ अखंड सत्य वचन बोलसी ॥ आतां जावें हरिकथेसी ॥ आपुले बिऱ्हाडासी घेऊनि ॥ ७७ ॥ आह्मां सकळांसी आला टणक ॥ आतां निद्रा करितों देख ॥ तरी बिऱ्हाड पाहूनि आणिक ॥ दुकान तेथें ठेवीं कां ॥ ७८ ॥ येथें तस्कर पडलिया पाहीं ॥ तरी आमुचे अंगीं शब्द नाहीं ॥ कीर्तनांत पडतें पदरीं कायी ॥ तें आह्मांसी कांहीं कळेना ॥ ७९ ॥ भानुदास उत्तर देत पाहा हो ॥ बिऱ्हाड जावो अथवा राहो ॥ परी पांडुरंगीं जडला भावो ॥ तो मी सर्वथा न सोडीं ॥ ८० ॥ ऐसें बोलोनि वैष्णवभक्त ॥ बिऱ्हाड टाकोनि गेला त्वरित ॥ कीर्तनीं बैसले साधुसंत ॥ तेथें त्वरित पातला ॥ ८१ ॥ अति उल्हास धरूनि मानसीं ॥ नमस्कार केला हरिदासांसी ॥ ह्मणे धन्य पर्वकाळ एकादशी ॥ क्षेम संतांसी दिधलें ॥ ८२ ॥ रामकृष्णचरित्र तारक जनीं ॥ वैष्णव गाती प्रेमेंकरूनी ॥ तें भानुदास आवडीकरूनी ॥ ऐकती श्रवणीं निजप्रेमें ॥ ८३ ॥ इकडे व्यवसायी दुर्मती ॥ बिऱ्हाडीं बैसोनि विचार करिती ॥ कीं भानुदास गेला कीर्तनाप्रती ॥ बिऱ्हाड

निश्चितीं टाकूनि ॥ ८४ ॥ तरी आतां करूनियां युक्त ॥ अश्व सोडोनि द्यावा त्वरित ॥ दिंड टाकावें गारींत ॥ तयासी मात न कळतां ॥ ८५ ॥ तो आपणासी पुसेल जर ॥ तरी त्यासी सांगावें आले तस्कर ॥ आम्हांसी निद्रा लागली फार ॥ तों गेले सत्वर न कळतां ॥ ८६ ॥ मग तो घरासी जाईल परतोन ॥ आपण कापड घेऊं वांटोन ॥ ऐसा विचार करूनि दुर्जन ॥ अश्व सोडून दिधला ॥ ८७ ॥ गर्ता पडली होती थोर ॥ त्यामाजी दिंड टाकिलें सत्वर ॥ टाळिया पिटोनि येरयेर ॥ देती उत्तर एकमेकां ॥ ८८ ॥ भानुदास लागला आमुचे संगतीं ॥ तैं पासोनि त्यासी आली संपत्ती ॥ दरिद्र आलें आम्हांप्रती ॥ ग्राहिक जाती त्याकडे ॥ ८९ ॥ ते सर्व चिंता आजि निरसली ॥ औषधावांचोनि खरूज गेली ॥ ऐसी एकमेकांसी बोली ॥ दुर्जनीं मांडिली तेधवां ॥ ९० ॥ धर्माची हिरून घेतां संपत्ती ॥ जैसा दुर्योधन उल्हासला चित्तीं ॥ तैसे ते व्यवसायी दुर्मती ॥ संतोष मानिती निजमनीं ॥ ९१ ॥ ऐसा अपाय देखोनि त्वरित ॥ सत्वर पावले रुक्मिणीकांत ॥ ह्मणे भानुदास बैसला कीर्तनांत ॥ निश्चळ चित्त करूनि ॥ ९२ ॥ दुर्मती मिळोनि अवघे जण ॥ गर्तेमाजी टाकिलें दुकान ॥ आतां विचार करावा कवण ॥ जगज्जीवन ह्मणतसे ॥ ९३ ॥ अश्व जाईल एखादीकडे ॥ मग तो पाहील कोणीकडे ॥ त्याणें प्रपंचाची टाकूनि चाड ॥ लाविलें वेड मद्भ-जनीं ॥ ९४ ॥ ऐसें ह्मणोनि पंढरीनाथ ॥ विप्रवेष धरिला त्वरित ॥ अश्व पाहूनि बाजारांत ॥ धरूनि बैसत तेधवां ॥ ९५ ॥ जो क्षीर-सागरीं शेषशयन ॥ ज्याचे लक्ष्मी ध्यातसे चरण ॥ तो भक्तकैवारी मनमोहन ॥ अश्व धरून बैसला ॥ ९६ ॥ योगी बैसले समाधीसी ॥ त्यांच्या लवकरी न ये ध्यानासी ॥ तो भक्तकैवारी हृषीकेशी ॥ धरूनि अश्वासी बैसला ॥ ९७ ॥ व्रतें तीर्थें तपें योग ॥ करितां नातुडे श्रीरंग ॥ तो पुंडलीकवरद पांडुरंग ॥ अश्व धरून बैसला ॥ ९८ ॥ जो विरिंचीचा निजजनिता ॥ अनंत ब्रह्मांडांचा कर्ता ॥ तो भानुदासाचा

अश्व जातां ॥ धरूनि चोहटा बैसला ॥ ९९ ॥ व्यवसायी बैसले देउळांत ॥ ते भानुदासाची निंदा करीत ॥ ह्मणती आतां येईल अकस्मात ॥ दुकान त्वरित पाहावया ॥ १०० ॥ येथील वृत्तांत कळतां सकळ ॥ मग करीत बैसेल तळमळ ॥ ऐसें परस्परें बोलती खळ ॥ ऐकोनि घननीळ कोपला ॥ १ ॥ अवकृपा करितां जगज्जीवन ॥ तों अकस्मात तस्कर आले जाण ॥ व्यवसायांचें दुकान लुटून ॥ केलें ताडन सकळांसी ॥ २ ॥ सकळ घोडीं सोडोनि नेलीं ॥ मग रडत बैसले तये वेळीं ॥ म्हणती भानुदासाची छळणा केली ॥ ते प्रचीत दाविली पांडुरंगें ॥ ३ ॥ एक म्हणती ये संधी ॥ कर्मासारिखी होतसे बुद्धी ॥ आपण ज्ञानहीन त्रिशुद्धी ॥ विचार आधीं न केला ॥ ४ ॥ एक म्हणती प्राक्तन खोटें ॥ म्हणोनि कर्म घडलें ओखटें ॥ भानुदास भक्त एकनिष्ट ॥ केली कटकट व्यर्थ तयासी ॥ ५ ॥ दीर्घस्वरें रडती जाण ॥ कोणी नगरांतूनि न ये धांवून ॥ तो मायालाघवी रुक्मिणीरमण ॥ घातलें मोहन सकळांसी ॥ ६ ॥ इकडे कीर्तनीं होय आनंदगजर ॥ मृदंग विणे वाजती सुस्वर ॥ तेणें नादें कोंदलें अंबर ॥ होत गजर नामाचा ॥ ७ ॥ चार घटिका यामिनी उरली होती ॥ तेव्हां वैष्णवीं केली आरती ॥ भावें ओंवाळूनि रुक्मिणीपती ॥ खिरापती वांटिल्या ॥ ८ ॥ नमस्कारूनि हरिदासासी ॥ भानुदास चालिले बिऱ्हाडासी ॥ तंव एक ब्राह्मण अश्वापासीं ॥ धरूनि वाटेसी बैसला ॥ ९ ॥ सन्निध चालोनि जातांचि पाहीं ॥ अश्व हिंसला ते समयीं ॥ म्हणे आपुला अश्व ये ठायीं ॥ कैसा आला कळेना ॥ १० ॥ तंव त्याचे गळ्यांत आंगवस्त्र घालून ॥ धरूनि बैसला एक ब्राह्मण ॥ तो भानुदासासी देखतांचि जाण ॥ अदृश्य झाला ते ठायीं ॥ ११ ॥ ऐसें कौतुक देखोनि सत्वरीं ॥ विस्मित झाला निजअंतरीं ॥ मग अश्व धरूनि निजकरीं ॥ भानुदास बिऱ्हाडीं पातले ॥ १२ ॥ तों व्यवसायी आपुले सांगाती ॥ दीर्घस्वरें रुदन करिती ॥ वृत्तांत पुसतां तयांप्रती ॥ मग ते सांगती सकळिक ॥ १३ ॥ आम्ही दुर्बुद्धि भाग्यहीन ॥

करूं पातलों तुझें छळण ॥ गर्तेमाजी दिंड टाकून ॥ अश्व सोडून दिधला ॥ १४ ॥ मग दोन प्रहर भरतां निशी ॥ तस्करीं लुटिलें आम्हांसी ॥ प्राक्तनाची गती ऐसी ॥ कोणापासीं सांगावें ॥ १५ ॥ घोडीं दिंडें गेलीं समस्त ॥ आणि मारही बसला अपरिमित ॥ पुढें संसाराची मात ॥ खुंटली निश्चित दिसताहे ॥ १६ ॥ आमुचें भांडवल बुडोनि गेलें ॥ तुझें ईश्वरें वाचविलें ॥ पैलगर्तेमाजी टाकिलें ॥ तें सांभाळिलें पाहिजे ॥ १७ ॥ ऐसें वचन ऐकूनि सत्वर ॥ भानुदासाचें द्रवलें अंतर ॥ म्हणे अश्व धरूनि रुक्मिणीवर ॥ बैसले असतील वाटतें ॥ १८ ॥ मग म्हणे रे कटकटा ॥ प्रपंचव्यवहार करितों खोटा ॥ तेथें आत्मसुखाचा नाहीं सांठा ॥ व्यर्थ करंटा भुललों मी ॥ १९ ॥ सांवळा सुकुमार राजीवनयन ॥ पीतांबरधारी जगज्जीवन ॥ तो मजसाठीं विप्रवेष धरून ॥ अश्व धरून बैसला ॥ १२० ॥ जेणें शीण आला पंढरीनाथा ॥ तें कर्म आतां न करावें सर्वथा ॥ ऐसा अनुताप धरूनि चित्ता ॥ जाहला बोलता तयांसी ॥ २१ ॥ व्यवसायांसी म्हणे भानुदास ॥ आतां स्वस्थ करावें मानस ॥ तस्करीं दंडिलें तुम्हांस ॥ तरी खेद चित्तास न करावा ॥ २२ ॥ गर्तेंतून दिंड काढोनी ॥ वस्त्रें दिधलीं तयांसी वांटोनी ॥ अश्व द्रव्य त्यांसी अर्पूनी ॥ भानुदास तेथोनि निघाले ॥ २३ ॥ निजमंदिरासी जाऊन ॥ करीत बैसला हरिभजन ॥ टाकोनियां मानाभिमान ॥ कीर्तनीं गुण गातसे ॥ २४ ॥ न करी कोणाचें उपार्जन ॥ प्रपंचचिंतेंत न घाली मन ॥ कुटुंब कलत्र असोन ॥ उदासपणें वर्ततसे ॥ २५ ॥ आषाढी कार्तिकी येतां बरी ॥ चालवी पंढरीची वारी ॥ टाळ-मृदंग-घोषगजरीं ॥ कीर्तन करी वाळुवंटीं ॥ २६ ॥ नानापरींची कवित्वकळा ॥ रचूनि आळवी घनसांवळा ॥ हृदयीं प्रेमाचा जिव्हाळा ॥ कीर्तनीं गळा सद्गदित ॥ २७ ॥ भानुदास कीर्तनीं उभे राहती ॥ तेव्हां स्वानंदजळें नेत्र भरती ॥ ते आवडी देखोनि रुक्मिणीपती ॥ नृत्य करिती त्या ठायीं ॥ २८ ॥ दुर्बुद्धि अथवा अज्ञान खळ ॥

तेहि ऐकूनि होती प्रेमळ ॥ म्हणती तया मुखींचें कीर्तन प्रांजळ ॥ सर्व काळ ऐकावें ॥ २९ ॥ कैची लटकी प्रपंचमाया ॥ कैची नाशवंत काया ॥ ऐसें ज्ञान होऊनि श्रोतयां ॥ धरिती दया सर्वांभूतीं ॥ १३० ॥ अयाचित वृत्तीकरून ॥ कोणी देईल वस्त्र अन्न ॥ परी स्वमुखेंकरूनि जाण ॥ नाहीं मागणें कोणासी ॥ ३१ ॥ आपलें आणि पराव ॥ हे कल्पनाचि नाहीं स्वभाव ॥ सर्वांभूतीं ऐक्यभाव ॥ विकल्पभाव टाकिला ॥ ३२ ॥ यापरी भानुदासाचें चित्त ॥ सदा सर्वकाळ वैराग्य भरित ॥ प्रेमउल्हासें दिवसरात ॥ भजन करीत श्रीहरीचें ॥ ३३ ॥ पुढिले अध्यायीं जगदुद्धारा ॥ राजा नेईल विद्यानगरा ॥ ते सुरस कथा ऐकतां चतुरा ॥ उल्हास अंतरा वाटेल ॥ ३४ ॥ संतसज्जन दैवतमेळीं ॥ महाराष्ट्र ओंव्या फुलें मोकळीं ॥ महीपति घेऊनि पुष्पांजळी ॥ उभा जवळीं तिष्ठत ॥ ३५ ॥ स्वस्ति श्रीभक्तविजय ग्रंथ ॥ ऐकतां तुष्टेल जगन्नाथ ॥ प्रेमळ ऐका भाविक भक्त ॥ द्विचत्वारिंशाध्याय रसाळ हा ॥ १३६ ॥ ॥श्रीकृष्णार्पणमस्तु॥ ॥अध्याय॥ ४२ ॥

अध्याय ४३ वा.

श्रीगणेशाय नमः ॥ श्रीवसुदेवनंदनाय नमः ॥ ऐका श्रोते सज्जन प्रेमळ ॥ आजि कल्पतरूसी पातलें फळ ॥ जे भक्तकथा अति रसाळ ॥ प्रकटल्या प्रांजळ निरुपम ॥ १ ॥ जो अनिर्वाच्य वैष्णवमहिमा ॥ विरिंचीसी न कळे ज्याची सीमा ॥ जयाचा पार नेणवे निगमा ॥ तो अनुपम प्रेमा जाणिजे ॥ २ ॥ जयांसी सत्कर्मचि प्रधान ॥ ते अंतीं पावती ब्रह्मभुवन ॥ जे यज्ञयाग आचरती जाण ॥ ते करिती गमन स्वर्गलोकीं ॥ ३ ॥ जे पितरांचे ठाईं भाव धरिती ॥ ते अंतीं पितृवासींच विचरती ॥ जे ज्या देवातें भजती ॥ तें पद पावती अंतीं ते ॥ ४ ॥ पिशाच

उपासिती तामसगुणी ॥ ते तैसेच होती देहांतीं मरणीं ॥ जे भक्तकथा ऐकती श्रवणीं ॥ ते वैकुंठभुवनीं पावती ॥ ५ ॥ त्यांचें संकट देखतां नयनीं ॥ तें तत्काळ निवारी चक्रपाणी ॥ अंतीं चतुर्भुजरूप करूनी ॥ सायुज्यसदनीं बैसवी ॥ ६ ॥ ऐसा वर पंढरीनाथें ॥ दिधला असे या ग्रंथातें ॥ ह्मणोनि श्रोते सादर चित्तें ॥ ऐका श्रवणार्थ निजप्रीतीं ॥ ७ ॥ मागील अध्यायाचे अंतीं ॥ भानुदासास भेटले रुक्मिणीपती ॥ मग त्याणें धरून विरक्ती ॥ प्रपंचवृत्ति सांडिली ॥ ८ ॥ आतां ऐका यावरी निरूपण ॥ पंढरीक्षेत्रींचा एक ब्राह्मण ॥ द्रव्यइच्छा मनीं धरून ॥ देशावरासी चालिला ॥ ९ ॥तो पुरें पट्टणें पाहतां सत्वरा ॥ अकस्मात आला विद्यानगरा ॥ नगरीं प्रवेशोनि सत्वरा ॥ म्हणे नृपवरा भेटावें ॥ १० ॥ स्नानसंध्या करूनि द्विजवर ॥ मग प्रवेशला राजमंदिर ॥ परी द्वारपाळ जाऊं न देती सत्वर ॥ बैसा क्षणभर म्हणोनि ॥ ११ ॥ भूपतीची आज्ञा आणितों सत्वर ॥ मग प्रवेशा जी नृपमंदिर ॥ रायासी पुसोनि आले किंकर ॥ मग भीतरीं द्विजवर प्रवेशला ॥ १२ ॥ ब्राह्मणास देखोनि रामराजा ॥ नमन करूनि केली पूजा ॥ अति उल्हास वाटला द्विजा ॥ म्हणे धन्य महाराजा धर्ममूर्ति ॥ १३ ॥ राजा पुसे त्याजकारण ॥ कोठोनि जाहलें जी आगमन ॥ काय मनीं इच्छा धरून ॥ कृपा करून आलेती ॥ १४ ॥ ऐसें पुसतां नृपनाथ ॥ ब्राह्मण सांगे उल्हासयुक्त ॥ म्हणे पंढरीक्षेत्र अति अद्भुत ॥ वास्तव्य तेथें असे कीं ॥ १५ ॥ तुझें औदार्य ऐकोनि सत्वर ॥ पाहावयासी आलों देशावर ॥ वचन ऐकोनि नृपवर ॥ संतोष थोर वाटला ॥ १६ ॥ राजा म्हणे ब्राह्मणासी ॥ तुम्हीं असावें स्वस्थ मानसीं ॥ मी स्नान करूनि त्वरेंसीं ॥ देवीपूजनासी जाईन ॥ १७ ॥ तुम्हीं तेथें येऊनि पाहावें स्थळ ॥ सुवर्णकांति असे देऊळ ॥ मी अर्चन करूनि सकळ ॥ तुलसीदल अर्पीन ॥ १८ ॥ ऐसें बोलतां तयाप्रति ॥ द्विज संतोष पावला चित्तीं ॥ देवीदर्शना चालिला भूपती ॥ त्याचे संगतीं जातसे ॥ १९ ॥ देवा-

लयाभोंवतीं असोलिका ॥ रायें लाविली पुष्पवाटिका ॥ अंतरगाभारीं स्थापूनि अंबिका ॥ समारंभ निका करीतसे ॥ २० ॥ नानावाद्यांचे होती गजर ॥ पूजा करीत बैसला नृपवर ॥ द्विज बोलती मंत्रोच्चार ॥ आनंदें गजर होतसे ॥ २१ ॥ षोडशोपचारें करूनि पूजनें ॥ देवीस लेववी वस्त्रें भूषणें ॥ नानापरींचीं दिव्य रत्नें ॥ शोभायमान दिसती पैं ॥ २२ ॥ चंदनादिक उपचार ॥ कंठीं घातले सुमनहार ॥ धूप दीप करूनि नृपवर ॥ नैवेद्य भावें अर्पितसे ॥ २३ ॥ मग पंचारती उजळोनियां ॥ ओंवाळिली महामाया ॥ साष्टांग नमस्कार घालोनियां ॥ लागला पायां नृपनाथ ॥ २४ ॥ प्रसाद वांटोनियां सकळांसी ॥ राजा बैसला स्वस्थ मानसीं ॥ मग पंढरीच्या द्विजासी ॥ बोलता झाला तेधवां ॥ २५ ॥ म्हणे राजाईऐसें दैवत पाहीं ॥ धुंडितां त्रिभुवनीं न दिसे कांहीं ॥ आम्हीं देखिलें ऐकिलें नाहीं ॥ धन्य नवाई अगाध ॥ २६ ॥ सुंदर देऊळ पाहावें नयनीं ॥ यासी रुप्याचें सारिलें पाणी ॥ भोंवतीं पुष्पवाटिका लावूनी ॥ पूजितों सुमनीं जगदंबा ॥ २७ ॥ विद्यानगरींचे सकळ जन ॥ येती घ्यावया दर्शन ॥ सेवेसी लाविले प्रधानजन ॥ मी निजांगें पूजन करीतसें ॥ २८ ॥ तुम्ही राहतां पंढरीसी ॥ तेथें तों महिमा नसेल ऐसी ॥ राजाईऐसे पांडुरंगासीं ॥ उपचार तयासी नसतील ॥ २९ ॥ दुर्बळ ब्राह्मण करिती पूजन ॥ तेथें कैंचें वस्त्र भूषण ॥ ऐकोनि रामरायाचें वचन ॥ विप्र निजमनीं क्रोधावला ॥ ३० ॥ मग म्हणे गा नृपनाथा ॥ पंढरी दृष्टीस न देखतां ॥ आपुलीच थोर म्हणसी देवता ॥ अभिमान वृथा धरूनि ॥ ३१ ॥ देउळासी रुप्याचें दिधलें पाणी ॥ तेंचि भूषण सांगसी जनीं ॥ आमुचें क्षेत्र सुवर्णकोंदणीं ॥ गेला रचोनि विश्वकर्मा ॥ ३२ ॥ तेथें कल्पतरूचीं लागलीं झाडें ॥ परीस चिंतामणि लोळती खडे ॥ दिव्य पताका चहूंकडे ॥ चपळेऐशा फडकती ॥ ३३ ॥ तेथें कामधेनूंचीं गोधन ॥ रत्नजडित वृंदावन ॥ तेथें प्रेमळ वैष्णवजन ॥ करिती कीर्तन उल्हासें ॥ ३४ ॥ तेथें चंद्रभागा

अमृतवाहिनी ॥ जे सकळ तीर्थांची स्वामिनी ॥ दर्शनेंचि मुक्त होती प्राणी ॥ वैकुंठभुवनीं पावती ॥ ३५ ॥ रंभा तिलोत्तमा येऊनि सुंदरी ॥ नृत्य करिती गरुडपारीं ॥ गंधर्वगायन होतसे द्वारीं ॥ नाद अंबरीं कोंदाटे ॥ ३६ ॥ ऐसा देवाधिदेव रुक्मिणीकांत ॥ क्षीरसागरीं होता नांदत ॥ तो पुंडलीक देखोनि निजभक्त ॥ आला त्वरित त्या ठाया ॥ ३७ ॥ दोनी कर ठेवूनि जघनीं ॥ उभा राहिला चक्रपाणी ॥ निज-भक्तांचें संकट देखोनी ॥ पावे ते क्षणीं निजांगें ॥ ३८ ॥ त्याचें स्वरूप पाहतां नयनीं ॥ लक्ष्मी लज्जित जाहली मनीं ॥ कोटिसूर्य जाती लपोनी ॥ मुकुटावरूनि तयाच्या ॥ ३९ ॥ सांवळा सुकुमार शार्ङ्गधर ॥ कांसे कसिला पीतांबर ॥ दिव्य कुंडलें मकराकार ॥ श्रीमुख मनोहर साजिरें ॥ ४० ॥ हें रूप देखावया दृष्टीं ॥ इंद्रादि देव तेतीस कोटी ॥ कर जोडोनि सदा तिष्ठती ॥ सद्भावें स्तविती निजप्रेमें ॥ ४१ ॥ ज्याचें नाम अहर्निशीं ॥ एकांतीं जपे कैलासवासी ॥ श्रुतिशास्त्रें वर्णिती जयासी ॥ पार विरिंचीसी नेणवे ॥ ४२ ॥ सहस्रमुखें स्तवन प्रीतीं ॥ शेष करिता जाहला निगुतीं ॥ जिव्हा चिरूनि दुखंड होती ॥ मग निवांतस्थिति राहिला ॥ ४३ ॥ पांडुरंगाऐसें दैवत ॥ आणि पंढरीऐसें पुण्यक्षेत्र ॥ चंद्रभागेऐसें पावन तीर्थ ॥ नाहीं दिसत त्रिभुवनीं ॥ ४४ ॥ हें दृष्टीस आधीं न पाहतां ॥ आपुलेंच भूषण सांगसी वृथा ॥ राजाई तुझी कुळदेवता ॥ हे माझिया चित्ता न ये कीं ॥ ४५ ॥ हे नित्य पंढरीस येऊन ॥ करीतसे सडासंमार्जन ॥ ऐसें बोलतांचि ब्राह्मण ॥ क्रोधायमान नृपनाथ ॥ ४६ ॥ ह्मणे माझी आराध्यदेवता ॥ याणें निंदिली मजदेखतां ॥ आपुलीच सांगे प्रशंसावार्ता ॥ विचार चित्ता न करितां ॥ ४७ ॥ आतां जीवें मारावें यासी ॥ तरी अधिकारी व्हावें दोषासी ॥ शिक्षा करूनि द्विजासी ॥ नगरप्रदेशीं दवडावा ॥ ४८ ॥ मग ब्राह्मणासी ह्मणे नृपवर ॥ तूं असत्य बोलिलासी उत्तर ॥ सुवर्णमय पंढरपुर ॥ ऐकिलें साचार नाहीं कीं ॥ ४९ ॥ आणि राजाई दैवत मूळपीठवासी ॥ इजला

स्वमुखें ह्मणतोसी दासी ॥ तरी शिक्षा करूनि तुजसी ॥ अरण्यासी दवडीन ॥ ९० ॥ मग ब्राह्मण ह्मणे ऐक भूपती ॥ म्यां यथार्थ सांगितलें तुजप्रती ॥ तुह्मी पंढरीस येऊन सत्वरगती ॥ रुक्मिणीपति पहावा ॥ ९१ ॥ म्यां सांगितलें त्याचें महिमान ॥ त्याहूनि विशेष कोटिगुण ॥ तुझे दृष्टीस न पडतां जाण ॥ मग दंडन करावें ॥ ९२ ॥ तो देवाधिदेव देखिला नाहीं ॥ तोंवरींच थोर हे राजाई ॥ जैसा सूर्योदय न होतांचि पाहीं ॥ दीपक सोज्वळ दिसती ॥ ९३ ॥ जों देखिला नाहीं ऐरावती ॥ तों इतर वारण थोर भासती ॥ कीं पौर्णिमेचा नुगवतां निशापती ॥ उडुगणें वाटती सतेज ॥ ९४ ॥ नातरी सुधारस न येतां हाता ॥ इतर रसांची तंवचि वार्ता ॥ कीं पयोब्धि दृष्टीस न देखतां ॥ दिसती सरिता अनुपम ॥ ९५ ॥ कल्पतरूचें न देखतां वन ॥ तोंवरीं आवडे आंबेवन ॥ ऐकिलें नाहीं वेदांतज्ञान ॥ तोंवरी पाखंडगान आवडे ॥ ९६ ॥ देखिला नाहीं सुवर्णपर्वत ॥ तोंवरींच पितळ झगमगित ॥ तेवीं जों देखिला नाहीं पंढरीनाथ ॥ तों इतर दैवतें आवडती ॥ ९७ ॥ ऐकोनि ह्मणे नृपवर ॥ आतां पंढरीस येतों सत्वर ॥ सांगितल्याऐसें देखिलें जर ॥ तरीच बरें द्विजवरा ॥ ९८ ॥ आणि असत्य वदलें असेल जरी ॥ तरी शिक्षा करीन तुज सत्वरीं ॥ मग प्रधानासी सांगे ते अवसरीं ॥ करावी स्वारी निजांगें ॥ ९९ ॥ अश्व गज रथ शिबिकाभरण ॥ सवें घेऊनि कांहीं सैन्य ॥ राजा सत्वर चालिल जाणा ॥ पांडुरंगदर्शन घ्यावया ॥ १०० ॥ नानावाद्यांचे होताती गजर ॥ तयांमागून चाले द्विजवर ॥ ह्मणे लज्जा रक्षील रुक्मिणीवर ॥ कीं करील अव्हेर दीनाचा ॥ १०१ ॥ म्यां सांगितलें जैशा रीतीं ॥ तैसें न देखे जरी भूपती ॥ तरी शिक्षा करील मजप्रती ॥ संशय चित्तीं न धरितां ॥ १०२ ॥ मग ध्यानीं आणोनि पांडुरंगमूर्ती ॥ स्तवन करी आपुले चित्तीं ॥ ह्मणे भक्तवत्सला रुक्मिणीपती ॥ मज या आकांतीं पावावें ॥ १०३ ॥ अनाथ दीन तुझा ब्राह्मण ॥ देशावरासी निघालों जाण ॥ तुझें सांगूनि नामामि-

धान ॥ कुटुंबरक्षण करीतसें ॥ ६४ ॥ देवा तुझी अद्भुत कीर्ती ॥
वर्णिली आहे मागिल्या संतीं ॥ तैसीच सांगितली रायाप्रती ॥ परी
यथार्थ चित्तीं वाटेना ॥ ६५ ॥ त्याची निंदिली कुळदेवता ॥ ह्मणोनि
राग आला नृपनाथा ॥ साक्ष पाहावयासी आतां ॥ पंढरीनाथा येतसे
॥ ६६ ॥ पंढरी आहे जैशा रीतीं ॥ तैसेंच कथिलें रायाप्रती ॥ परी
कलियुगीं मृत्तिकेच्या भिंती ॥ लोकांसी भासती अभिन्नत्वें ॥ ६७ ॥
जैसें वडिलांचें द्रव्य पुरल असे ॥ तें निर्दैव्यासी पाहतां दिसती कोळसे ॥
तैसीच पंढरी सुवर्णमय असे ॥ परी विकल्पें न दिसे सर्वथा ॥ ६८ ॥
संतीं मागें केली कथनी ॥ म्यां तैसेंचि सांगितलें त्यालागोनी ॥ आतां
दृष्टीस न देखतां चक्रपाणी ॥ तरी मजलागोनि दंडील तो ॥ ६९ ॥
मग मी आपुला देईन प्राण ॥ परी असत्य होईल संतवचन ॥ पुढें पंढरी-
माहात्म्य ऐकोनि सज्जन ॥ विश्वास मनीं न धरितील ॥ ७० ॥ अनाथ-
नाथा रुक्मिणीवरा ॥ ऐशा संकटीं पाव सत्वरा ॥ करुणा भाकितां
द्विजअंतरा ॥ जगदुद्धारा जाणवलें ॥ ७१ ॥ ह्मणे माझी कीर्ति वाखा-
णितां गहन ॥ ब्राह्मणाचा होतो अपमान ॥ तरी जैसें कथिलें आहे
तयान ॥ तैसेंच दाखवणें लागेल ॥ ७२ ॥ ऐसा स्वमनीं करूनि विचार ॥
रुक्मिणीसी सांगे शार्ङ्गधर ॥ विद्यानगरींचा नृपवर ॥ येतो सत्वर दर्शना
॥ ७३ ॥ तरी जैसी होती द्वारकापुरी ॥ त्याहूनि विशेष आहे पंढरी ॥
नृपवरासी दाखवूं निमिषभरी ॥ संशय निवारूं तयाचा ॥ ७४ ॥ नाहीं
तरी शिक्षा पावेल ब्राह्मण ॥ मग तो देईल आपुला प्राण ॥ आणि
आपुलें बिरुदासी येईल उण ॥ संतसज्जन हांसतील ॥ ७५ ॥ वचन
ऐकोनि जगज्जननी ॥ चरण नमस्कारी तये क्षणीं ॥ ह्मणे वैकुंठींची
रचना आणोनी ॥ रायासी ये क्षणीं दाखवीन ॥ ७६ ॥ ऐसी कल्पना
करितां जाण ॥ तैसेंचि जाहलें न लागतां क्षण ॥ तो मायालाघवी जग-
ज्जीवन ॥ निजभक्तमहिमान वाढवी ॥ ७७ ॥ तों इकडे रामराजा चालतां
सत्वर ॥ सन्निध उरलें पंढरपुर ॥ भयभीत होऊनि द्विजवर ॥ रुक्मिणीवर

आळवीतसे ॥ ७८ ॥ मग सन्निध पाचारून द्विजा ॥ काय बोलतसे रामराजा ॥ आतां संशय न फिटतां माझा ॥ तरी अपमान तुझा करीन ॥ ७९ ॥ मग सन्निध वारण आणवूनि त्वरित ॥ अंबारींत बैसला नृपनाथ ॥ पंढरी विलोकितांचि त्वरित ॥ तों नवल अद्भुत देखिलें ॥ ८० ॥ जैसा पौर्णिमेचा निशापती ॥ त्याभोंवतीं नक्षत्रें दिसती ॥ तेवीं देवालयाच्या कळसाभोंवतीं ॥ मंदिरें चमकती लखलखीत ॥ ८१ ॥ हें कौतुक देखतां दृष्टीसी ॥ राजा विस्मित जाहला मानसीं ॥ ह्मणे ब्राह्मणें कथिली जैसी ॥ पंढरी तैसी दिसताहे ॥ ८२ ॥ मग अनुताप धरून चित्तांत ॥ खालीं उतरला नृपनाथ ॥ नमस्कार साष्टांग घालूनि त्वरित ॥ विप्रासी बोलत तेधवां ॥ ८३ ॥ तुम्हीं सांगितलें जैशा रीतीं ॥ तैसेंच दिसोन येतसे पुढती ॥ मी नेणतां अभिमान धरूनि निश्चितीं ॥ विकल्प चित्तीं धरियेला ॥ ८४ ॥ ऐसें बोलोनि नृपवर ॥ द्विजासी केला नमस्कार ॥ मग शुद्ध करूनि अभ्यंतर ॥ चरणीं सत्वर लागला ॥ ८५ ॥ ब्राह्मण विस्मय पावला चित्तीं ॥ म्हणे मज पावला रुक्मिणीपती ॥ हर्ष न मावे त्रिजगतीं ॥ गातसे कीर्ति सप्रेम ॥ ८६ ॥ भक्तांमाजी अग्रगणी ॥ एक पुंडलीक शिरोमणी ॥ त्याचे भेटीसी द्वारकेहूनी ॥ चक्रपाणि पातले ॥ ८७ ॥ सकळ तीर्थांत वरिष्ठ गंगा ॥ तीहूनि विशेष चंद्रभागा ॥ दर्शनेंच पावन करी जगा ॥ अभिमान अंगा जडों नेदी ॥ ८८ ॥ मथुरा गोकुळ वृंदावन ॥ ये स्थळीं नांदे जगज्जीवन ॥ द्वारकेंतही श्रीकृष्ण ॥ भक्तांकारण तिष्ठत ॥ ८९ ॥ परी या क्षेत्रींचें महिमान ॥ अनुपम दिसतसे मजलागून ॥ ऐसा ब्राह्मण निर्लज्ज होऊन ॥ गातसे गुण निजप्रीतीं ॥ ९० ॥ टाळ मृदंग आणोनि त्वरित ॥ समारंभ करी नृपनाथ ॥ मिळवूनियां वैष्णवभक्त ॥ गजर करित स्वानंदें ॥ ९१ ॥ पुढें विलोकितांचि जाण ॥ तों कल्पतरूंचें लागलें वन ॥ खडे परीस चिंतामणीसमान ॥ लागतां रान पंढरीचें ॥ ९२ ॥ कामधेनूऐशा उदंड गायी ॥ भोंवत्या असती तये ठायीं ॥ राजा विस्मित होऊनि पाही ॥

ह्मणे धन्य नवायी अगाध ॥ ९३ ॥ ब्राह्मणाचा धरूनि हात ॥ भूपति पुढें विलोकित ॥ तों पंढरीक्षेत्र लखलखित ॥ पाहतां दिपत नेत्रपातीं ॥ ९४ ॥ तरूवरी बैसोनि पक्षियाती ॥ निजच्छंदें गायन करिती ॥ हंस मयूर नृत्य करिती ॥ सप्रेम गाती उल्हासें ॥ ९५ ॥ तपस्वी करिती अनुष्ठान ॥ ब्राह्मण करिती वेदाध्ययन ॥ विष्णुभक्त करिती कीर्तन ॥ मृदंग विणे घेऊनि ॥ ९६ ॥ ठायीं ठायीं सभा करूनि जाणा ॥ नृत्य करिती देवांगना ॥ तेणें तटस्थता येऊनि नयना ॥ विषयिक जना भुलविलें ॥ ९७ ॥ संत बैसोनि ठायीं ठायीं ॥ आत्मचर्चा बोलती पाहीं ॥ अनुभवें तल्लीन होऊनि तेही ॥ आलिंगन देती येरयेरां ॥ ९८ ॥ चंद्रभागेसी अष्टोत्तर शत ॥ तीर्थें येऊनि मूर्तिमंत ॥ स्नान करूनि पावन होत ॥ दृष्टीस पाहात नृपनाथ ॥ ९९ ॥ एक कनकाचें रचून वृंदावन ॥ त्यावरी बैसविलें रत्नकोंदण ॥ दिव्य लेवूनि वस्त्राभरण ॥ करिती पूजन नरनारी ॥ १०० ॥ मग भीमरथींत करूनि स्नाना ॥ राजा चालिला देवदर्शना ॥ तों इंद्रादिदेव सकळ जाणा ॥ पंढरीराणा लक्षिती ॥ १ ॥ अष्टसिद्धि सकळ दासी ॥ निजांगें राबती देवापासीं ॥ तयांमाजी अकस्मात राजाईसी ॥ रायें दृष्टीसी ओळखिलें ॥ २ ॥ ह्मणे विद्यानगरीं अर्चितों पूजनीं ॥ तेचि हे आमुची कुळस्वामिनी ॥ ती पंढरीस झाडीतसे अंगणीं ॥ विस्मित मनीं नृपनाथ ॥ ३ ॥ उदो शब्द ह्मणोनि ते समयीं ॥ राजा तीस पुसे लवलाहीं ॥ ह्मगे माते तूं किमर्थ ये ठायीं ॥ निजांगें पाहीं झाडितेसी ॥ ४ ॥ मग भवानी उत्तर देत तयासी ॥ तुवां व्यर्थचि अहंता धरिली मानसीं ॥ मजऐशा अनंत दासी ॥ येती पंढरीसी राबावया ॥ ५ ॥ या पुंडलिकाचे अंगणीं ॥ सकळ तीर्थें घालिती लोळणी ॥ मग पवित्र होऊनि तत्क्षणीं ॥ वाहाती पाणी निजांगें ॥ ६ ॥ विस्मित होऊनि नृपनाथ ॥ पुढें विलोकूनि जों पाहात ॥ तों नारद तुंबर येऊन तेथ ॥ कीर्तन करित देखिले ॥ ७ ॥ चतुर्भुजरूपें नारीनर ॥ अवघे दिसती साकार ॥ लोटांगण घाली नृपवर ॥ स्वानंदें निर्भर मानसीं

॥ ८ ॥ शंखचक्रादि आयुधें घेऊनी ॥ द्वारीं जय विजय तिष्ठती दोनी ॥ दिव्य पताका गगनीं ॥ चपळेऐशा झळकती ॥ ९ ॥ मागुती घालोनि दंडवत ॥ राजा प्रवेशला राउळांत ॥ तें तेज पाहतां नेत्र झांकत ॥ मग धरिला हस्त ब्राह्मणाचा ॥ ११० ॥ तों सांवळा सुकुमार राजीवनयन ॥ पीतांबरधारी जगज्जीवन ॥ कमललोचन सुहास्यवदन ॥ स्वरूप सगुण देखिलें ॥ ११ ॥ जें योगियांचें निजध्यान ॥ हृदयीं ध्यातो पंचवदन ॥ तें स्वरूप वर्णितांचि जाण ॥ उपमा गौण दिसताहे ॥ १२ ॥ अमृताची चवी सांगतां ॥ उपमा द्यावया रस कोणता ॥ तेवीं देवाधिदेव रुक्मिणी-कांता ॥ दृष्टांतीं वर्णितां न ये कीं ॥ १३ ॥ तरी दृष्टीस देखती निज-भक्तजन ॥ तेचि अनुभवें जाणती खूण ॥ येरवीं बुद्धिमंत करितां स्तवन ॥ पडलें मौन श्रुतीसी ॥ १४ ॥ ऐसी निरुपम परब्रह्ममूर्ती ॥ प्रीतीनें आलिंगी भूपती ॥ स्वरूप न्याहाळूनियां दिठीं ॥ मग चरणीं मिठी घातली ॥ १५ ॥ ब्राह्मणासी ह्मणे रामराजा ॥ तूं सखा सद्गुरु जिवलग माझा ॥ काय उपकार आठवूं तुझा ॥ गरुडध्वजा भेटविलें ॥ १६ ॥ तुवां जें कां कथिलें देख ॥ त्याहूनि कोटिगुणें अधिक ॥ दृष्टीं देखिला वैकुंठनायक ॥ सौख्य अनेक पावलों ॥ १७ ॥ राजाई माझी कुळ-स्वामिनी ॥ तेही झाडितां देखिली अंगणीं ॥ इंद्रासमवेत सुर येउनी ॥ कर जोडोनि तिष्ठती ॥ १८ ॥ पंढरीऐसें क्षेत्र अद्भुत ॥ आणि पांडु-रंगाऐसें वरिष्ठ दैवत ॥ चंद्रभागेऐसें पावन तीर्थ ॥ नाहीं दिसत त्रिभुवनीं ॥ १९ ॥ धुंधरडें होतां उंबराआड ॥ तें ह्मणे माझें हें ब्रह्मांड गाढ ॥ फोडोनि दाखवितां चहूंकडे ॥ होतसे वेडें निजमनीं ॥ १२० ॥ तैसेंचि जाहलें रायाकारण ॥ मग ब्राह्मणाचे धरिले चरण ॥ ह्मणे मी वेष्टिलों होतों अविद्येंकरून ॥ परी जाहलों पावन तुझेनी ॥ २१ ॥ यापरी कौतुक दाखवूनि जाणा ॥ मग अदृश्य जाहली तितुकीही रचना ॥ तों मृत्तिकेच्या भिंती दिसती नयना ॥ आश्चर्य मनांत वाटत ॥ २२ ॥ जैसें दाखविलें रायाप्रती ॥ तैसेंच पंढरीक्षेत्र आहे निश्चितीं ॥ परी मनुष्यासी

मृत्तिकाऐसी भासती ॥ निजकर्मगतीकरूनि ॥ २३ ॥ सांप्रत आपण। जैसें दिसत ॥ तैसेंच देखे नृपनाथ ॥ विस्मित होऊनि मनांत ॥ ह्मणे चमत्कार बहुत देखिला ॥ २४ ॥ राजा विचारी आपुले मनीं ॥ आतां व्यर्थ कासया पुजावी भवानी ॥ सन्निध क्षीरसागर टाकूनि ॥ सरिता-जीवनीं कां न्हावें ॥ २९ ॥ अमृतसरोवर देखिल्या पाहीं ॥ दिव्य औषधी कासया घ्यावी ॥ कल्पतरु सन्निध असोनि पाहीं ॥ बाभूळछायीं न बैसावें ॥ २६ ॥ हातींचा परीस टाकोनियां ॥ धातुवादी व्हावें कासया ॥ कामधेनु गृहासी आलिया ॥ अजा कासया पुजावी ॥ २७ ॥ गृहीं प्रकटतां सूर्यनारायण ॥ मग दीप कासया सरसावण ॥ तेवीं जाहलिया पांडुरंगदर्शन ॥ देवीउपासन कासया ॥ २८ ॥ ऐसें ह्मणोनि रामराजा ॥ प्रार्थितसे गरुडध्वजा ॥ ह्मणे देवाधिदेवा वैकुंठराजा ॥ मनोरथ माझा पुरवीं कां ॥ २९ ॥ चित्तीं हेत आहे ऐसा मजला ॥ कीं विद्यानगरासी न्यावें तुजला ॥ आतां अभय देऊनि शरणागताला ॥ सत्वर चला देवराया ॥ १३० ॥ देव ह्मणे भूमीवरी ठेवितां मजसी ॥ तरी तेथेंच राहीन निश्चयेंसी ॥ कांहीं अन्याय घडतां तुजसी ॥ मागुती पंढरीसी येईन ॥ ३१ ॥ ऐसें सांगतां चक्रपाणी ॥ राजा हर्षला आपुले मनीं ॥ म्हणे स्थळोस्थळीं डांक ठेवूनी ॥ जाईन घेऊनि देवासी ॥ ३२ ॥ पंढरीक्षेत्रापासूनि जाण ॥ विद्यानगरापर्यंत तेण ॥ दों भागीं मनुष्यें उभीं करून ॥ मूर्ति काढून नेतसे ॥ ३३ ॥ पुजारी ब्राम्हण निवांत ठायीं ॥ भूपतीसीं बळ न चले कांहीं ॥ मूर्ति उचलोनि लवलाहीं ॥ हातोहातीं चालिले ॥ ३४ ॥ विद्यानगरासी नेऊनि सवेग ॥ तेथें स्थापिला पांडुरंग ॥ नानापरींचे उपचारभोग ॥ राजा निजांगें करीतसे ॥ ३९ ॥ इकडे यात्रेसी आषाढमासीं ॥ वैष्णव आले पंढरीसी ॥ तेथें मात ऐकिली ऐसी ॥ कीं विद्यानगरासी देव गेले ॥ ३६ ॥ उदास दिसे पंढरपुर ॥ जैसें प्राणावांचोनि शरीर ॥ कीं सरितेमाजी नसतां नीर ॥ जेवीं भयासुर वाटे ते ॥ ३७ ॥ कीं नृपावांचोनि सैन्यसंपत्ती ॥ कीं चंद्रावांचोनि

नक्षत्रजाती ॥ नातरी भ्रताराविण पतिव्रता सती ॥ निढळ दिसती जनांत ॥ ३८ ॥ तेवीं विद्यानगरासी गेलिया हरि ॥ अवघी उदास दिसे पंढरी ॥ संतमहंत गरुडपारीं ॥ येऊनि सत्वरीं बैसले ॥ ३९ ॥ म्हणती कोणाचें करावें कीर्तन ॥ आम्हांसी टाकिलें जगज्जीवनें ॥ पुंडलीकासी दिधलें वरदान ॥ तें असत्य वचन जाहलें कीं ॥ १४० ॥ भाविक भक्त आले सर्व ॥ म्हणती काय जाहला पंढरीराव ॥ विद्यानगरासी गेले देव ॥ कळला अभिप्राव सकळांसी ॥ ४१ ॥ संतसाधु वैष्णवजन ॥ एकमेकांसी बोलती वचन ॥ विद्यानगरासी कोणी जाऊन ॥ रुक्मिणीरमण आणावा ॥ ४२ ॥ ऐसें एकमेकांसी बोलती वचन ॥ परी कोणीच न देती आश्वासन ॥ म्हणती पुंडलिकासी गेला उपेक्षून ॥ तो आमुचेन न ये सर्वथा ॥ ४३ ॥ एक बोलती प्रत्युत्तरीं ॥ आमुचा प्रवेश नोहे राजमंदिरीं ॥ नृपास वृत्तांत कळेल जरी ॥ तरी शिक्षा बरी करील कीं ॥ ४४ ॥ एक दाविती निर्गुणभाव ॥ आपुले देहींच आहे देव ॥ चित्तीं नसतांचि अनुभव ॥ बोलती वाव आत्मज्ञानी ॥ ४५ ॥ एक म्हणती ईश्वरइच्छेन ॥ जें जें जैसें येईल घडोन ॥ तें तें दृष्टीं पाहावें आपण ॥ तळमळ कोणी न करावी ॥ ४६ ॥ त्यांत भानुदास वैष्णवभक्त ॥ प्रतिज्ञा करूनि काय बोलत ॥ मी घेऊनि येतों रुक्मिणीकांत ॥ नाहीं तरी जीवित न ठेवीं ॥ ४७ ॥ ऐसें बोलोनि तयांप्रति ॥ तेथोनि निघाला सत्वरगती ॥ विद्यानगरासी जाऊन रातीं ॥ लोकांप्रति पुसतसे ॥ ४८ ॥ पंढरीहूनि पांडुरंगमूर्ती ॥ येथें घेऊनि आला नृपती ॥ ते कोठें स्थापिली निश्चितीं ॥ सांगा मजप्रति लवलाहें ॥ ४९ ॥ राजयाच्या भयेंकरून ॥ कोणी यथार्थ न सांगती वचन ॥ आम्हांसी विदित नाहीं म्हणोन ॥ प्रतिवचन बोलती ॥ १५० ॥ मग भानुदास पुसती एकांतीं ॥ त्यांस सांगितलें वैष्णवभक्तीं ॥ मंदिरीं ठेवूनि रुक्मिणीपती ॥ पूजी एकांतीं नृपनाथ ॥ ५१ ॥ राजा करूनि गेलिया पूजन ॥ मग आणिकासी नव्हे दर्शन ॥ कपाटें कुलपें घालून ॥ द्वारपाळ

रक्षणा ठेविले ॥ ९२ ॥ ऐसी ऐकोनिया मात ॥ भानुदास झाला हर्षयुक्त ॥ मग अर्धरात्र लोटतांचि त्वरित ॥ झाले निद्रित सकळिक ॥ ९३ ॥ द्वारापासीं येतांचि जाण ॥ कुलुपें गळालीं न लागतां क्षण ॥ भानुदास आंत प्रवेशोन ॥ घातलें नमन साष्टांग ॥ ९४ ॥ स्वरूप दृष्टीसीं न्याहाळून ॥ आलिंगन दिधलें प्रीतींकरून ॥ कंठ सद्गदित होऊन ॥ देवासी विनवण करीतसे ॥ ९५ ॥ म्हणे लक्ष्मीकांता वैकुंठवासिया ॥ पुंडलीकवरदा यादवराया ॥ आम्हांवरी लोभ सांडोनिया ॥ जाहलासी रायास्वाधीन ॥ ९६ ॥ पुंडलिकासी दिधलें वरदान ॥ कीं कदापि न जाय येथून ॥ तें तुझें आतां अभयवचन ॥ असत्य दिसोन आलें कीं ॥ ९७ ॥ आम्हां दुर्बळांची नावडे पूजा ॥ येथें उपचार करितो राजा ॥ तें सुख मानोनि अधोक्षजा ॥ गरुडध्वजा राहिलासी ॥ ९८ ॥ दिव्य वस्त्रें आणि आभरण ॥ नैवेद्यासी अनेक पक्वान्न ॥ यालागीं दुर्बळांचें स्मरण ॥ तुजकारण नव्हे कीं ॥ ९९ ॥ रुक्मिणी राधा सत्यभामा ॥ इतुक्यांसी सांडोनि पुरुषोत्तमा ॥ रामरायें तुज लावूनि प्रेमा ॥ मेघश्यामा चालविलें ॥ १६० ॥ सांडोनियां पंढरपुर ॥ वसतें केलें विद्यानगर ॥ तेथें वाट पाहाती ऋषीश्वर ॥ भक्त थोर तिष्ठती ॥ ६१ ॥ रंभा तिलोत्तमा उर्वशी मेनका ॥ सेवेसी येती अष्टनायिका ॥ सांडोनियां विधिजनका ॥ बैसलासी निका ये ठायीं ॥ ६२ ॥ कीं आमुचे पदरीं दोष दारुण ॥ पळोनि आलासी तयाभेण ॥ कीं तुज मागतसों प्रेमदान ॥ म्हणोनि पळून आलासी ॥ ६३ ॥ कीं कीर्तनाचा होतो गलबला ॥ तेणें निद्रा न लागेची तुजला ॥ म्हणोनि एकांतीं ठाव पाहिला ॥ कळलें मजला यथार्थ ॥ ६४ ॥ कीं यात्रा मिळते असंख्यात ॥ तयांसी भेटतां शिणसी बहुत ॥ मग येऊनि विद्यानगरांत ॥ घेतोसी विश्रांति या ठायीं ॥ ६५ ॥ ऐकोनि भानुदासाचें वचन ॥ काय बोलतसे जगज्जीवन ॥ तूं बोलतोसी उदासवचन ॥ विचार मनीं न करितां ॥ ६६ ॥ मज न रुचती नाना उपचार ॥ वस्त्रें भूषणें अलंकार ॥ कधीं

देखेन भीमातीर ॥ म्हणोनि अंतर झुरतसे ॥ ६७ ॥ रायें आणोनि मजलागूनी ॥ येथें घातलें बंदिखानीं ॥ तुम्हींही निष्ठुर होऊनि मनीं ॥ परत कोणीं न केली ॥ ६८ ॥ ऋद्धि सिद्धि चारी मुक्ती ॥ मी देत होतों तुम्हांप्रती ॥ परी त्यांसी अव्हेरूनि निश्चितीं ॥ भजन प्रीतीं करीतसां ॥ ६९ ॥ याविरहित तों मजपासीं ॥ कांहींच न दिसे द्यावयासी ॥ सेवाऋण न फिटे मजसीं ॥ म्हणोनि तुम्हांसी टाकिलें ॥ १७० ॥ ऐसें बोलोनि रुक्मिणीकांत ॥ कंठ जाहला सद्गदित ॥ आनंदाश्रु नेत्रीं वाहात ॥ दोघेही स्फुंदत निजप्रेमें ॥ ७१ ॥ भानुदासासी जगज्जीवनें ॥ मागुती दिधलें आलिंगन ॥ म्हणे प्रातःकाळीं करितां पूजन ॥ देईन दर्शन तुजलागीं ॥ ७२ ॥ मग नवरत्नांचा काढोनि हार ॥ भानुदासासी देत शार्ङ्गधर ॥ म्हणे आतां बिऱ्हाडासी जाई सत्वर ॥ येईल नृपवर दर्शना ॥ ७३ ॥ बाहेर येतांचि भानुदास ॥ कुलुपें बैसलीं कवाडास ॥ अणुमात्र न कळतां कोणास ॥ निजभक्तास भेटला ॥ ७४ ॥ प्रातःकाळीं उठोनि नृपती ॥ स्नान केलें सत्वरगती ॥ देवासी नमन करूनि प्रीतीं ॥ कांकडआरती करीतसे ॥ ७५ ॥ तों कंठीं न दिसे रत्नहार ॥ पुजाऱ्यासी पुसिलें सत्वर ॥ ह्मणे येथें कोण आला तस्कर ॥ ह्मणोनि नृपवर क्रोधावला ॥ ७६ ॥ तयांसी ताडन करूनि बहुत ॥ ह्मणे हार त्वरीत आणिजे येथ ॥ अमूल्य रत्नें न मिळती निश्चित ॥ पृथ्वी समस्त धुंडितां ॥ ७७ ॥ ऐसी आज्ञा होतांचि सत्वर ॥ झाडा घेती घरोघर ॥ परी कोठेंचि न दिसे हार ॥ मग पाहाती बाहेर तस्करासी ॥ ७८ ॥ तों गंगातीरीं स्नान करूनी ॥ भानुदास बैसले नामस्मरणीं ॥ राजदूत पाहती विलोकूनी ॥ तों हार दुरूनि देखिला ॥ ७९ ॥ म्हणती सांपडला रे तस्कर ॥ आतां यास धरावा सत्वर ॥ अकस्मात बांधोनि वैष्णववीर ॥ चालले किंकर रायाचे ॥ १८० ॥ नगरांत आणितां त्याकारण ॥ देखोनि हांसती सकळ जन ॥ ह्मणती हा भोंदावया जनांकारण ॥ संत होऊन हिंडतो ॥ ८१ ॥

देवावरी हात घातला पाहें ॥ तो मनुष्यासी भियेल काय ॥ कसाबासी भेटतां कपिला गाय ॥ तो पूजील काय तिजलागीं ॥ ८२ ॥ ऐसें नानापरींचे त्रिविध जन ॥ भानुदासासी निंदिती देखोन ॥ परी तो खेद् न करी जाण ॥ नामस्मरण करीतसे ॥ ८३ ॥ एक ह्मणती मैंदाच्रिया गळां ॥ अहाणा बोलती तुळसीमाळा ॥ तो आजि प्रत्यक्ष देखीला डोळां ॥ हार चोरिला येणेंचि ॥ ८४ ॥ नवरत्नांचा हार घेऊन ॥ दूतांनीं रायासी दिधला नेऊन ॥ म्हणती तस्कर आणिला बांधोन ॥ तयासी दंड कोण करावा ॥ ८५ ॥ सक्रोध बोले नृपवर ॥ त्यास शूळावरी घाला सत्वर ॥ कोण कैसा पाहावा तस्कर ॥ ऐसा विचार न केला ॥ ८६ ॥ भानुदास दूतांसी बोले वचन ॥ माझें तंव सन्निध आलें मरण ॥ शेवटीं पांडुरंगाचें दर्शन ॥ मजकारण करवावें ॥ ८७ ॥ त्यांत कोणी होते सज्जन ॥ त्यांस मानलें त्याचें वचन ॥ मग रायासी आज्ञा मागून ॥ गेले घेऊन देऊळासी ॥ ८८ ॥ भानुदास ह्मणे देवाप्रती ॥ मी न्यावयासी आलों एकांतीं ॥ म्हणोनि योजिली ऐसी युक्ती ॥ आणि नृपाहातीं दंडविलें ॥ ८९ ॥ जो न्यावया येईल तुजकारण ॥ त्याचा ऐसाच ध्यावा प्राण ॥ मग राजमंदिरीं विलास भोगून ॥ सुखें राहावें या ठायीं ॥ १९० ॥ ऐसा विचार करूनि घननीळा ॥ मग हार घातला माझिया गळां ॥ ऐसें बोलतां तये वेळां ॥ अश्रु डोळां लोटले ॥ ९१ ॥ परी शतसहस्त्र जन्मांअंतीं ॥ तुज मी न सोडीं रुक्मिणीपती ॥ ऐसें बोलोनि मागुतीं ॥ नमन प्रीतीं घातलें ॥९२॥ दूत म्हणती ते अवसरीं ॥ आतां ऊठ गा चाल झटकरी ॥ आधींच केली नसती चोरी ॥ तरी ऐसी परी कां होती ॥ ९३ ॥ ऐसें म्हणोनि सत्वर ॥ भानुदासासी काढिलें बाहेर ॥ शूळ देऊनि खांद्यावर ॥ माथां शेंदूर घातला ॥ ९४ ॥ कौतुक पाहावया सत्वरीं ॥ अमित मिळाल्या नरनारी ॥ मग नेऊनि नगराबाहेरी ॥ शूळ झडकरी रोंविला ॥ ९५ ॥ उचलूनि जों घालावें वरी ॥ तों भानुदास देवातें विनंति करी ॥ म्हणे

आकाश कडकडोनि पडो मजवरी ॥ तरी तुज अंतरीं आठवीन ॥ ९६ ॥ सप्त समुद्र समरस जाहलिया ॥ तरी तुज न सोडीं देवराया ॥ तुजवरूनि नाशवंत काया ॥ ओवाळूनियां सांडिली ॥ ९७ ॥ लया जाईल सकळ क्षिती ॥ आणि पंचभूतेंही प्रळया पावती ॥ तैं तुजवांचूनि रुक्मिणीपती ॥ आणिक सांगाती असेना ॥ ९८ ॥ वडवानल खाईल त्रिभुवन ॥ तैं तूं माझा जिवलग प्राण ॥ भानुदासाचा निश्चय देखोन ॥ जगज्जीवन पावले ॥ ९९ ॥ तंव नवल वर्तलें अति अद्भुत ॥ तें सादर परिसा भाविक भक्त ॥ शूळ रोंविला होता जेथ ॥ त्यासी पल्लव अकस्मात फूटले ॥ २०० ॥ फुलें फळें आलीं बहुत ॥ राजासी जाऊनि सांगती मात ॥ ह्मणे तो आहे वैष्णवभक्त ॥ पंढरीनाथ पावला त्या ॥ १ ॥ शूळाचा वृक्ष जाहला सत्वर॥ राजासी सांगते जाहले किंकर ॥ वचन ऐकूनिया नृपवर ॥ आश्चर्य थोर करितसे ॥ २ ॥ पहावयासी येतां त्वरित॥ तंव दृष्टीस देखिलें साक्षात ॥ मग अनुताप पावला चित्तांत ॥ ह्मणे अन्याय बहुत मज घडला ॥ ३ ॥ भानुदासासी नमस्कार प्रीतीं ॥ सद्भावें घालीतसे नृपती ॥ ह्मणे अपराध घडला मजप्रती ॥ विवेक चित्तीं न करितां ॥ ४ ॥ मग रामरायें भानुदासाप्रती॥ देउळीं नेला सत्वरगती ॥ दृष्टीस देखतां पांडुरंगमूर्ती ॥ सद्गदित कंठीं जाहला ॥ ५ ॥ चरणीं मिठी घालितांचि जाण ॥ उचलोनि धरी जगज्जीवन ॥ भानुदासासी ह्मणे रुक्मिणीरमण ॥ मजकारण शिणलासी ॥ ६ ॥ आतां मज घेऊनि खांद्यावरी ॥ पंढरपुरासी चाल सत्वरी ॥ तेथें पुंडलिकाचे द्वारीं ॥ निरंतरीं वसेन ॥ ७ ॥ रामराजा धरितसे पाय ॥ मज उपेक्षूनि जातां काय ॥ देव ह्मणती तुझा अन्याय ॥ घडोनि आला अनायासें ॥ ८ ॥ कांहीं तुझें होतें सुकृत ॥ ह्मणोनि होतों दिवस बहुत ॥ आतां माझें रूप हृदयांत ॥ आठवीं नित्य सप्रेम ॥ ९ ॥ भानुदास ह्मणे रुक्मिणीकांता ॥ कैसा उचलसील

मज आतां ॥ माझी तों नाहीं राजसत्ता ॥ म्यां मेळवूनि बहुतां तुज न्यावें ॥ २१० ॥ ऐकोनि म्हणे दीनदयाळ ॥ मी तुझे स्वाधीन जहालों केवळ ॥ आतां माझी सत्ता आहे सकळ ॥ ते तुझीच असे निजभक्ता ॥ ११ ॥ ऐसें ह्मणोनि जगज्जीवनें ॥ तत्काळ रूप धरिलें सान ॥ भानुदासासी बोले वचन ॥ सांबळींत घालोन मज नेईं ॥ १२ ॥ मग गवाळें आणोनि तयेक्षणीं ॥ त्यांत बांधिले चक्रपाणी ॥ ऐसी ऐकोनियां वाणी ॥ आशंकित मनीं न व्हावें ॥ १३ ॥ जैसे आकाश विस्तीर्ण आहे बहुत ॥ परी घटीं पाहतां तेवढेंच होत ॥ तेवीं भक्तलीलेसी वैकुंठनाथ ॥ सूक्ष्म होत निजप्रीतीं ॥ १४ ॥ कीं अफाट समीर आहे बहुत ॥ परी विंजणा हालवितां तैसाचि होत ॥ तेवीं भक्तां स्वाधीन रुक्मिणीकांत ॥ तैसाचि होत निजछंदें ॥ १५ ॥ मागें कृष्णावतारीं यशोदा घुसळितां ॥ जो डेरियामाजी लागला तिच्या हाता ॥ तो भानुदासाच्या गवाळ्यांत जातां ॥ संशय कोणता आणावा ॥ १६ ॥ जो अनंत घटीं व्यापून जाण ॥ तैसाचि दिसे थोर सान ॥ अणुरेणूपरीस लहान ॥ ज्ञानदृष्टीनें दिसताहे ॥ १७ ॥ तो भानुदासाचे आवडीसाठीं ॥ सांबळींत मावला जगजेठी ॥ खांद्यावरी घेऊनि उठाउठी ॥ सत्वरगती जातसे ॥ १८ ॥ मंजुळ शब्द गवळ्यांतून ॥ भक्तासी बोले जगज्जीवन ॥ धन्य आजिचा उगवला सुदिन ॥ संतसज्जन भेटतील ॥ १९ ॥ पद्मालयासी आले भानुदास ॥ तेथें खालीं ठेविला जगन्निवास ॥ आपण लागले स्नानास ॥ हर्ष चित्तास वाटला ॥ २२० ॥ इकडे सांबळींत होते रुक्मिणीवर ॥ ते एकाएकीं झाले थोर ॥ वरील पूड मस्तकावर ॥ तळींचा चूर झाला कीं ॥ २१ ॥ भानुदास येऊनि जंव पाहे ॥ ह्मणे देवाधिदेवा हें केलें काये ॥ थोर झालासी लवलाहें ॥ आतां उचलसील काय मजलागीं ॥ २२ ॥ मग ह्मणे रुक्मिणीवर ॥ तूं पुढें जाऊन सांग सत्वर ॥ नानावाद्यांचा

करूनि गजर ।। येतील सामोरे संतसाधु ।। २३ ।। सुदिनघटिका आजिचे दिनीं ।। मज बैसवावें सिंहासनीं ।। ऐसें बोलतां चक्रपाणी ।। भानुदास तेथुनि निघाला ।। २४ ।। तों गरुडपारीं वैष्णवभक्त ।। अवघे बैसले चिंताक्रांत ।। ह्मणती भानुदासासी दिवस लागले बहुत ।। परी रुक्मिणीकांत न ये कीं ।। २५ ।। तों अकस्मात भक्त विजयी ।। हास्यवदन त्यांहीं पाहीं ।। येतां देखिला लवलाहीं ।। ह्मणती शेषशायी आणिला ।। २६ ।। संतांसी क्षेम देऊनि त्वरित ।। ह्मणे पद्मालयासी आले रुक्मिणीकांत ।। ऐसी ऐकोनि हर्षमात ।। संतोषे चित्त सकळांचें ।। २७ ।। दिंडी पताका घेऊनि सत्वर ।। सामोरे चालिले वैष्णववीर ।। टाळमृदंगांचा गजर ।। वाद्यें अपार वाजती ।। २८ ।। पुजारी आणि लोकपाळ ।। नरनारी सामोरे जाती सकळ ।। पद्मालयासी येतां ते वेळ ।। देखिला घननीळ दृष्टींसी ।। २९ ।। सकळीं घालोनि दंडवत ।। देवासी आलिंगन देऊनि त्वरित ।। रथावरी बैसवोनि रुक्मिणीकांत ।। चालिले मिरवीत संभ्रमें ।। २३० ।। संत गर्जती गुणानुवाद ।। त्यांपुढें नट नाचती छंद ।। भेरी वाजंत्रांचा नाद ।। वाटतो आनंद सकळांसी ।। ३१ ।। तो समारंभ वर्णितां वाचेसीं ।। दृष्टांत न पुरे द्यावयासी ।। आतां प्रत्यक्ष कार्तिकमासीं ।। पाहाती दृष्टीसी वारकरी ।। ३२ ।। रथोत्साह पौर्णिमेसी होत ।। तेचि उपमा तया सरस ।। तैशाचपरी पंढरीनाथ ।। येती मिरवत निजछंदें ।। ३३ ।। येतां चंद्रभागेचें तीरीं ।। तंव ते पुढारी येत सामोरी ।। देवासी स्नान घालोनियां झडकरी ।। मग महाद्वारीं चालिले ।। ३४ ।। रथाखालीं उतरून सांवळी मूर्ती ।। शिबिकेंत घातली हातोहातीं ।। देवालयी नेऊन सत्वरगती ।। अभिषेक करिती मधुपर्क ।। ३५ ।। ब्राह्मण बोलती मंत्रघोष ।। कीर्तनीं गर्जती वैष्णवदास ।। सिंहासनी बैसे जगन्निवास ।। धन्य दिवस सुदिन तो ।। ३६ ।। वस्त्रालंकारभूषण ।। शोडषोपचारें

केलें पूजन ॥ पक्कान्न नैवेद्य अर्पून ॥ मंगलारती पैं केली ॥ ३७ ॥ पुष्पांजलि मंत्रघोष पुजारी समर्पिती देवास ॥ संत वैष्णव यात्रेकऱ्यांस ॥ वाटला उल्हास तेधवां ॥ ३८ ॥ नरनारी मिळोनि समस्त ॥ भानुदासाचें स्तवन करित ॥ ह्मणती याच्या योगें वैकुंठनाथ ॥ आले पंढरींत मागुती ॥ ३९ ॥ एक शर्करा नगरांत वांटिती ॥ एक पक्कान्नभोजन विप्रा घालिती ॥ क्षेत्रवासी लोकांप्रती ॥ आनंद चित्तीं वाटला ॥ ४० ॥ जैसा चतुर्दशवर्षें वनवास कंठोन ॥ अयोध्येसी आला रघुनंदन ॥ नगरवासी आनंदले जन ॥ तैसोंचि झालें तयांसी ॥ ४१ ॥ कीं अवर्षणीं अहाळला होता पर्वत ॥ त्यावरी मेघ वर्षला अपरिमित ॥ पंढरीचे लोक समस्त ॥ संतोष मानीत या रीतीं ॥ ४२ ॥ कीं अगस्तीच्या पोटांतूनी ॥ समुद्र निघाला देखूनि नयनीं ॥ मग मेघांसी उल्हास वाटला मनीं ॥ तैसीच करणी झाली कीं ॥ ४३ ॥ नातरी वसंतकाळ येतांचि त्वरित ॥ वनस्पती दिसती सुशोभित ॥ तेवीं पंढरीस येतां अनाथनाथ ॥ लोक समस्त आनंदले ॥ ४४ ॥ कीं शरीरांतील परतला प्राण ॥ मग इंद्रियें वर्तती सावधान ॥ पंढरीचे सकळही जन ॥ तैशाचपरी जाहले ॥ ४५ ॥ पुढिले अध्यायीं कथा सुरस ॥ ऐकतां यश जोडे निर्दोष ॥ ह्मणवूनि भक्त हो सावकाश ॥ जोड करा हेचि पैं ॥ ४६ ॥ हें सात्विक भक्तांचें महिमान ॥ वाढविता श्रीरुक्मिणीरमण ॥ महीपति त्याचा बंदीजन ॥ गातो सद्गुण कीर्तनीं ॥४७॥ स्वस्ति श्रीभक्तविजय ग्रंथ ॥ ऐकतां तुष्टेल जगन्नाथ ॥ प्रेमळ ऐका भाविक भक्त ॥ त्रिचत्वारिंशाध्याय रसाळ हा ॥ २४८ ॥

॥ अध्याय ॥ ४३ ॥ ॥ ओंव्या ॥ २४८ ॥

Appendix II

परिशिष्ट २.

विठ्ठलकविकृत भानुदासचरित्र.

(साक्या.)

यात्रा भरली पंढरपूरीं नाहीं पांडूरंग ।
म्हणती संतहि, 'कोठें गेला भक्तांचा भवभंग?' ॥ १ ॥
पडला संदेह सकळीकांसी, 'कां रे! उपेक्षा केली? ।
भेटी देईं' म्हणति, प्रभूला 'आम्ही दीन भुकेलीं.' ॥ २ ॥
विद्यानगरीं नेलें प्रभुला कळलें सर्व जनांला, ।
'आहा! दीनदयाळा! त्यजिलें, वाटे खेद मनाला.' ॥ ३ ॥
यापरि साधू तळमळती कीं चातक मेघालागीं, ।
खळवळलें पंढरपुर तेव्हां म्हणती 'आम्हि अभागी. ॥ ४ ॥
आहे ऐसा कोणि पराक्रमि भक्तशिरोमणि आतां ।
घेउनि येइल त्वरितचि येथें रखुमाईच्या कांता?' ॥ ५ ॥
कोणि न बोले मात ऐकुनी, म्हणती, त्यजिलें देवें, ।
करा प्रार्थना, कांहीं हरिच्या चुकलों असलों सेवे.' ॥ ६ ॥
भानुदास बोलिला समस्तां, 'मी आणिन भगवंता. ।
कैसा जाइल देव त्यजुनियां? सांडावी तुम्हि चिंता.' ॥ ७ ॥
नमन करुनियां मग सकळांसी भानूदास निघाला. ।
चाले चपळगतीनें तेव्हां विद्यानगरा आला. ॥ ८ ॥
जननी चुकतां तान्हें जैसें दीनपणानें पाहे, ।
त्यापरि भानूदास कृपाघन मंजुळवाणी बाहे. ॥ ९ ॥

वाजंत्र्यांच्या ध्वनी उमटती दुंदुभि वाजति नाना ।
दृष्टि पडेना कोठें हरि तो, करिती सुरस तनाना. ॥ १० ॥

प्रभातपूजा केलि नृपानें, न घडे कोणा भेटी, ।
सप्तहि द्वारें केलीं दृढतर, कुलुपानें जसि पेटी. ॥ ११ ॥

ऐसें कौतुक पाहुनि बोले भानुदास, 'श्रीरंगा! ।
बरा येउनी येथें बसलां सांडुनि सकळहि संगा ॥ १२ ॥

अम्हां अनाथां कोण पुसे? हरि! भाग्यवंत झालासी; ।
षड्रस अन्नें पाहुनि बरवीं भक्षाया आलासी. ॥ १३ ॥

आम्ही भक्त तुझे अतिदुर्बळ माळ बुका तुज वाहूं, ।
या रायाच्या उपचारातें स्वप्नीं कदापि न पाहूं. ॥ १४ ॥

यासाठीं तूं येथें लंपट होउनि राबसि, देवा!' ।
ऐसें म्हणतां भानूदासें काय वर्तलें तेव्हां. ॥ १५ ॥

झालि निशा, अति तमें दाटलीं, चिंता करि खगदास ।
जोडुनियां कर उभा तिष्ठतो 'चाल' म्हणे देवास. ॥ १६ ॥

'आतां न धरीं भीड तुझी मी, कां व्यालासी पोरें? ।
टाकुनि येतां लाज न धरिली, ऐसें न किजे थोरें. ॥ १७ ॥

आम्हांवांचुनि गति तुज नाहीं, लोकीं न करीं फजीती, ।
दुष्ट नष्ट लेंकुरें असति तरि त्यांतें काय त्यजीती?' ॥ १८ ॥

ऐसीं करुणावचनें ऐकुनि काय करी वनमाळी ।
बंधन केलीं होतिं कवाडें, उघडति लगबग टाळीं. ॥ १९ ॥

डोळे उघडुनि पाहे तेव्हां देखियलें भगवंता, ।
शिरला आंत, तसा मग बोले, 'हरली सकळहि चिंता.' ॥ २० ॥

साष्टांगें चरणांवरतें हा घालि मिठी रविदास ।
अश्रुजळानें पद प्रक्षाळी, आनंद हृदयास. ॥ २१ ॥

दोघां भेटी होतां बोले, 'कां पंढरिचा कंटाळा? ।
कां हो हरि बैसलां उगाचि? वश झालासि नृपाळा?' ॥ २२ ॥
देव म्हणे, 'मज बंदिं घातलें, अंतरलों शशिभागा, ।
भीमातिर पंढरपुरनगरी नाहिं असी दुजि जागा.' ॥ २३ ॥
यापरि हरि अनुवादुनियां मग काढी माळ गळ्याची ।
घाली भास्करदासा कंठीं आवडि रत्नफळांची. ॥ २४ ॥
बाहिर निघतां दास बोलिला, 'द्या मज भेट सकाळीं.' ।
उघडीं केलीं होतिं कवाडें, बसलीं दृढतर टाळीं. ॥ २५ ॥
प्रातःकाळीं स्नानालागीं भानुदास मग जात ।
आठवि अंतरिं कमळापतिला नाम मुखानें गात. ॥ २६ ॥
स्नान करुनियां घालुनि आसन निमग्न बसला ध्यानीं ।
ठेवुनियां चित्त पांडुरंगीं आळविला हरि त्यांनीं. ॥ २७ ॥
देवार्चन नृप करावयासी आला लगबग भारी ।
माळ पहातां न दिसे कंठीं ताडित फार पुजारी. ॥ २८ ॥
चोर पहाया धांवति सेवक शोध करिति गांवाचा ।
दासाकंठीं माळ पहातां 'चोर' म्हणति हा साचा. ॥ २९ ॥
ताडण करिती नृपसेवक त्या अणिला रायापाशीं ।
मग सक्रोधें बोले नृप तो, 'घाला शुळशिखराशी.' ॥ ३० ॥
चालविला मग शुळाजवळि तो म्हणे, 'ऐक नृपनाथा! ।
भेट घेउं दे मज देवाची, चरणीं ठेविन माथा.' ॥ ३१ ॥
येतां प्रभुसन्निध मग त्यानें नमन पदांबुजिं केलें ।
म्हणे, 'भला तूं पंढरिराया! बरें मला हित केलें. ॥ ३२ ॥
आतां देवा! लोभ असों द्या, आठव हृदयिं धरावा, ।
केली युक्ती तुम्हि मज कळलें भानूदास मरावा. ॥ ३३ ॥

परि तुज जन्मोजन्मि न सोडीं हा निश्चय भक्ताचा ।
असे; बरें त्वां केलें देवा! खेळ जसा वक्ताचा.' ॥ ३४ ॥
वेसीवरतीं शूल रोंविला, म्हणे, 'तयावरि घाला' ।
सच्चिद्धनसुख पूर्णकृपाकर आठवि हृदयिं निघाला. ॥ ३५ ॥
दासाचा करुणाकर तेव्हां कळवळला मनिं भारी ।
कंठ फूगला सद्गद, नेत्रीं वाहति मग निर्धारी. ॥ ३६ ॥
'गांजिल कोण बळी मम भक्तां?' धांवे हरि समयाला ।
सावरिवा अपुल्या वसनातें, धांवत हरिसम आला. ॥ ३७ ॥
पल्लव फुटले फळपुष्पांकित अकस्मात दिसताहे ।
सेवकजन सांगती नृपातें, जाउनी नेत्रीं पाहे. ॥ ३८ ॥
विस्मय वाटे सकळां चित्तीं रामराय पदिं लागे ।
जोडुनि करकमळांतें भानूदासा अभयचि मागे. ॥ ३९ ॥
आले पांडुरंगापाशीं दोघे भक्त, विनंती ।
करिते झाले, सद्गद तेव्हां कंठ, हरी करि खंती. ॥ ४० ॥
'कोणी माझा भक्त गांजिला सांगें भानूदासा?' ।
आलिंगुनियां देवें त्याप्रति तळमळि जैसा मासा. ॥ ४१ ॥
'आतां देवा! चला पंढरी, बैसुनियां मम खांदीं ।
नाहीं तर हा रामराय तुज काढिल युक्ति यखादि.' ॥ ४२ ॥
ऐकुनि ऐसी मात नृप म्हणे, 'कां हो! उपेक्षा माजी ।
करुनी जातां याजबराबर? त्यागुनि मजला आजी.' ॥ ४३ ॥
देव म्हणे, 'मी अपुल्या वचना सत्य करुनियां आतां ।
जातों, लोभ असों दे, मजवर क्षोभुं नको; नृपनाथा!' ॥ ४४ ॥
रविदासानें बसवुनि खांदीं, पंढरीस मग जात ।
भक्त धांवती देव पहाया 'आला' ऐकुनि मात. ॥ ४५ ॥

दिव्य पताका उभवुनि तेव्हां संत नाचती नाना ।
सर्वां अंतरिं हर्ष न माये करिती सुरस तनाना. ॥ ४६ ॥
लोक धांवती बहु नगरीचे लोळति दासापाईं ।
'धन्य धन्य तूं या लोकांतें दाविलि बहुत नवाई.' ॥ ४७ ॥
सर्व मिळुनियां देव बसविला नेवुनि आपुल्या गादी ।
भरली यात्रा फारचि तेव्हां गाती ऐकति नादी. ॥ ४८ ॥
कोणी करिती देवपूजना, कोणी नाचति छंदें, ।
कोणी भानूदास वर्णिती गाउनि गीत अनंदें. ॥ ४९ ॥
कोणी ऐकत बसले तेथें, कोणी पुराण वाची, ।
कोणी करिती स्नानें दानें, स्तुति करिती देवाची. ॥ ५० ॥

उपसंहार.

यापरि झाला मोद बहूतचि विठ्ठल केशवपायीं ।
दृढ जडला, मग संतचरित्रें भक्तांचे गुण गाई. ॥ ५१ ॥

Appendix III

परिशिष्ट ३

केशव स्वामीकृत श्री एकनाथस्वामींचें चरित्र

चतुर्दशीचें कीर्त्तन ॥ महाद्वारीं कीजे आपण ॥ हें पांडुरंग-आज्ञावचन ॥ प्रतिपाळण करावें ॥ ४३ ॥ कैसी आज्ञातीचें कारण ॥ सविस्तर सांगावें निरोपण ॥ ऐकतांचि श्रीनाथ प्रश्न ॥ चरित्र प्राचीन वर्णिती ॥ ४४ ॥ पूर्वीं कोण्हेकाळीं येथ ॥ चरित्र जालें अत्यद्भुत ॥ तें परिसावया श्रीनाथ ॥ देत चित्त सादरत्वें ॥ ४५ ॥ विद्यानगरीं राज्यप्राप्ती ॥ रामराजा भक्त मूर्ती ॥ अति भावार्थी विठ्ठल भक्तीं ॥ केली ख्याति नवलाव ॥ ४६ ॥ प्रार्थुनि पांडुरंगासीं ॥ म्हणे चलावें मम नगरासी ॥ धरणें बैसोनि दिवानिशीं ॥ करी उपवासासी सत्पात्र ॥ ४७ ॥ देव चित्ताचा कोंवळा ॥ आज्ञापिलें तयावेळां ॥ एके दिनीं आणि सोंवळा ॥ नेसी प्रेमळा तरीच घडे ॥ ४८ ॥ या दोन नेमा विरहित ॥ माझें येणें न घडे निश्चित ॥ रायें ऐकोनिया मात ॥ पडिला विचारार्थ यदर्थी ॥ ४९ ॥ बोलावूनि सुबुद्धि प्रधान ॥ सांगे कोडें देववचन ॥ प्रधानें विचारोनि मना ॥ म्हणे विज्ञापना अवधारीं ॥ ५० ॥ देवें घाळूनि कोडें प्रबळ ॥ पाहतसे तुझ्या भक्तीचें बळ येथें बुद्धि एकचि प्रांजळ ॥ ते निश्चळ परिसावी ॥ ५१ ॥ स्वराज्य देशांतील समस्त ॥ लहान थोर विप्र येथ ॥ आणवूनि सुनिश्चित ॥ विनीत व्रत विचारावें ॥ ५२ ॥ आलिया समस्तांच्या मना पंढरीहून स्वस्थाना ॥ पर्यंत तया ब्राह्मणां ॥ सोंवळेंचि जाणा उभे कीजे ॥ ५३ ॥ हातोहातीं देवासी ॥ देवोनियां सावकाशी ॥ अविश्रम एक्या दिवशीं ॥ स्वस्थानासी पैं न्यावें ॥ ५४ ॥ कुशळ बुद्धि ऐकोनि

कानीं ॥ राजा संतोषला मनीं ॥ त्वरें आज्ञापत्र देउनी ॥ दूतां लागुनी पाठविलें ॥ ५५ ॥ आपुल्या राज्यांतील ब्राह्मण ॥ समस्त लहान थोर आणुन ॥ अविनित मृदु प्रश्न ॥ हें कार्य आपण निवेदिलें ॥ ५६ ॥ राजआज्ञा आणि परमार्थ ॥ समस्त हे अंगिकारित ॥ दिवस एक नेमुनी त्वरित ॥ पंथीं राहवीत ग्रामांतरीं ॥ ५७ ॥ पंढरीहून स्थानपर्यंत ॥ अन्नोदक संस्था यथास्थित ॥ गांवोगांवीं करवी नृपनाथ ॥ अति विनीत द्विजभक्ती ॥ ५८ ॥ नेमले दिवशीं ब्राह्मण ॥ स्वस्थळीं करूनि स्नान ॥ मार्गावरी हो येऊन ॥ सोंवळेंच जाण उभे ठाकती ॥ ५९ ॥ राजा प्रधान पादचारी ॥ पंढरी प्रासादा भीतरीं ॥ येऊनि साष्टांग नमस्कारी ॥ विनंति करी देवासी ॥ ६० ॥ आज्ञेप्रमाणें निश्चिती ॥ सोंवळें ब्राह्मण उभे असती ॥ कृपा करोन शीघ्र गती ॥ चलावें म्हणती विठ्ठला ॥ ६१ ॥ विनवोनियां ऐशा रिती ॥ ब्राह्मणांसी म्हणे नृपती ॥ देवासी उचला हातोहातीं ॥ स्वस्थानाप्रती पाववा ॥ ६२ ॥ आग्रह करितां देव ॥ ब्राह्मणांसी उचले स्वयमेव ॥ हातोहातीं ब्राह्मण सर्व ॥ नेती नवलाव कौतुकें ॥ ६३ ॥ श्रम न होतां कोणासी ॥ देव नेऊन एक्या दिवशीं ॥ पावविला त्या स्थानासी ॥ निज नेमेसीं उचलोनी ॥ ६४ ॥ राजा येऊनि आपण ॥ रत्नजडित सिंहासन ॥ प्रासादें निजकरें मांडून ॥ वरीं स्थापना करी देवा ॥ ६५ ॥ नानावस्त्रें अलंकार ॥ सुवर्ण रत्नमय विचित्र ॥ गळां नवरत्नाचे हार ॥ शोभा अपार पैं केली ॥ ६६ ॥ षोडशोपचारी पूजा ॥ सुगंध द्रव्य अति वोजा ॥ पूजोनियां अधोक्षजा ॥ वाजंत्रबाजा गजरेसी ॥ ६७ ॥ समस्त ब्राह्मण संतर्पण ॥ यथाविधीं अति दिव्यान्न ॥ देऊनि तयां भोजन ॥ वस्त्र गौरवून अति प्रीती ॥ ६८ ॥ भिक्षुकांसी दक्षिणा दान ॥ देऊनि तोषविलें ब्राह्मण ॥ आशीर्वाद मुखें गर्जोन ॥ नृपतीसी पुसोन पैं गेले ॥ ६९ ॥ देव प्रासाद बळकट ॥ तीन पोंवळ्यासह कपाट ॥ कड्या कुलपें घनदाट ॥

केली खटपट दृढतेची ॥ ७० ॥ पूजेसीं नेमिले ब्राह्मण ॥ त्यांचा निर्वाह सहकुटुंब जाण ॥ कोणासीं न वाटे शीण ॥ तेचि संभावना करीतसे ॥ ७१ ॥ त्रिकाळीं पूजा नेमस्त ॥ साहित्य अति यथोक्त ॥ राजाही त्रिकाळ दर्शन घेत ॥ अति विनीत भक्तीसीं ॥ ७२ ॥ यापरि भाग्यविलास ॥ देव भोगी सावकाश ॥ येरीकडे पंढरीस ॥ यात्रा दिवस पैं आला ॥७३॥ वार्षिक यात्रेची यापरी ॥ यात्रा दाटली नरनारी ॥ सत्पुरुष मंडळी स्वनिर्धारीं ॥ आले पंढरी तें ऐका ॥७४॥ नामदेव अति आवडता॥ लडिवाळ देवाचा तत्वतां ॥ निवृत्ति ज्ञान सोपाननाथा ॥ देवही माथा वंदीतसे ॥ ७५ ॥ सांवता माळी कुंभार गोरा ॥ या भक्तांच्या मुख्य धुरा ॥ चोखामेळा अति शूद्रा ॥ संगें ढोरा वोढी देव ॥ ७६ ॥ ज्ञानी विसोबा खेचर ॥ नामदेवाचा गुरु साचार ॥ भानुदास अति प्रियकर ॥ आवडता फार देवाचा ॥ ७७ ॥ नामदेवाचे चौघे पुत्र ॥ आणिकही लहान थोर ॥ यात्रेसी मिळाले अपार ॥ करीत जयजयकार नामाचा ॥ ७८ ॥ तंव देव नेलियाची वार्ता ॥ बडवे सांगती उद्विग्नता ॥ निस्तेज पंढरी देखता ॥ सर्वांसी चिंत्ता पैं जाली ॥ ७९ ॥ बडवे म्हणती संतांप्रतीं ॥ तुम्हासारिख्या थोर मूर्ती ॥ असतां देव कळा हातीं ॥ हे ख्याति राजयाची ॥ ८० ॥ तंव निवृत्ति श्रीज्ञानदेव ॥ म्हणती नवल जालें अपूर्व ॥ धन्य नृपतीचें लाघव ॥ कैवारें देव पैं नेला ॥ ८१ ॥ नामा अथवा भानुदास ॥ अवश्य आणितील देवास ॥ बोलावूनियां उभयतांस ॥ या विचारास योजावें ॥ ८२ ॥ एक विचारें समस्त ॥ त्या उभयतां बोलावित ॥ देव आणिला पाहिजे त्वरित ॥ भक्तिभावार्थ प्रतापें ॥ ८३ ॥ तंव भानुदासें समस्तांसी ॥ वंदोनि अति उल्हासी ॥ म्हणे आज्ञाप्रतापें यशरासी ॥ घेऊनि देवासी येतसों ॥ ८४ ॥ मानलें सकळांच्या चित्तीं ॥ सन्मानूनि निरोप देती ॥ सत्य घेऊनि संतमूर्ती ॥ शीघ्र गति चालिला ॥ ८५ ॥ संत आणि यात्रा समस्त ॥ निवांत होऊनि वाट पाहात ॥

भानुदास नृप नगरांत ॥ पावोनि राहात दुकानीं ॥ ८६ ॥ तथील पाहिला वृत्तांत ॥ तंव देवासी अर्गळा बहुत ॥ कोणी नवा प्राणी तेथ ॥ आज्ञेविरहित जाऊं नपवे ॥ ८७ ॥ देव पडला बंदिखानीं ॥ भानुदास विव्हळ मनीं ॥ कार्य साधे कैसेनी ॥ आठवी मनीं विठ्ठल ॥ ८८ ॥ ऐशा परी चिंताक्रांत ॥ होता लोटली अर्ध रात्र ॥ भानुदास जंव लक्षित ॥ निवळ एकांत दिसतसे ॥ ८९ ॥ निद्रिस्थ जालें सकळ जन ॥ आतां पाहावा करूनि प्रयत्न ॥ दुकानींहूनि उठोन ॥ देवद्वारीं जाण पातला ॥ ९० ॥ कपाटासी लाविता हात ॥ तंव तें सहज मुक्त होत ॥ प्रवेश करुनी आंत ॥ मागुती लोटित कपाटां ॥ ९१ ॥ याचिपरी दुसरी पोवळीं ॥ कपाटां उघडी ते काळीं ॥ मुख्य प्रासादा जवळीं ॥ येऊन न्याहाळी कपाटा ॥ ९२ ॥ तंव लखलखाट तेजदीप्ती ॥ सुवर्ण बुटी भिंती शोभती ॥ कवाडेंही तोचि स्थिती ॥ दैदीप्य दिसती डोळियां ॥ ९३ ॥ भानुदासें स्पर्शितां हात ॥ मुख्य कपाट मुक्त होत ॥ हर्षयुक्त आनंद चित्त ॥ स्वयें जात भीतरीं ॥ ९४ ॥ कर्पूर दीपिका चहूं कोनीं ॥ लखलखाट उजेड नयनीं ॥ रत्नजडित सिंहासनीं ॥ देव चूडामणी विठ्ठल ॥ ९५ ॥ देखतांचि श्रीमूर्ती ॥ थोर आनंद जाला चित्तीं ॥ क्षुधे तृषेची खंती ॥ हरपोनी विश्रांति पावला ॥ ९६ ॥ पांडुरंगे अतितांतडी ॥ घातली सिंहासनाहुनी उडी ॥ भानुदास अति आवडी ॥ हृदयीं परवडी कवळिला ॥ ९७ ॥ बहुकाळें भेटतां बाळा ॥ मातेसी जैसा कळवळा ॥ अश्रुधारा स्रवती डोळां ॥ देव कोंवळा चित्ताचा ॥ ९८ ॥ भानुदासा पडले ठक ॥ तटस्थ ठेला क्षण एक ॥ देवें थापटूनि देख ॥ आलिंगूनि कौतुक पैं केलें ॥ ९९ ॥ सावध भानुदास होतां ॥ पायांवरी ठेवोनि माथा ॥ स्फुंदस्फुंदोनी आक्रंदतां ॥ प्रेमावस्था नावरे ॥ १०० ॥ कुरवाळोनी स्वहस्तें ॥ सुख अर्पी तयातें ॥ म्हणे आवरोनि प्रेमातें ॥ गुजहितातें बोलावें ॥ १ ॥ प्रेमावस्था जिरवोनि पोटीं ॥ सांगों लागे

गुजगोष्टी ॥ कार्य होतें जें पोटीं ॥ अभंग ओंठीं निघतसे ॥ २ ॥
॥ अभंग ॥ चंद्रभागा तिरीं उभा विटेवरी ॥ विठो राज्य करीं पंढरीये
॥ १ ॥ ऋद्धि सिद्धि वोळंगती परिवार ॥ न लाहती अवसर ब्रह्मादिक
॥ २ ॥ सांडूनि तितुके व्यर्थ वांझ केले ॥ कवणे चाळवीले काडिया
॥ ३ ॥ शंख भेरी मृदंग वाजती काहळा ॥ उपवड राउळा होतअसे ॥
॥ ४ ॥ चांपेल मार्जन सुगंध चर्चून ॥ भीमरा चंदन वाट पाहे ॥ ५ ॥
रंभा तिलोत्तमा उर्वशी मेनीका ॥ कामिनी आणिका येती सेवे ॥ ६ ॥
कनकाचे पर्यकीं रत्नाचे दीपक ॥ देखोनि श्रीमुख वोंवाळिती ॥ ७ ॥
रखुमाई आई ते जाली उदास ॥ कैसें पुंडलिकास मौन पडलें ॥ ८ ॥
भक्त भागवत सकळ पारुशले ॥ निःशब्दें ते ठेले तुजवीणें ॥ ९ ॥ धन्य
पंढरपूर विश्वाचें माहेर ॥ धन्य भीमातीर वाळुवंट ॥१०॥ भानुदास ह्मणे
चाल आह्मासवें ॥ वाचा ऋणदेवें आठवावें ॥ ११ ॥ ओवी ॥ यापरी
भांडूनि देवासी ॥ तेचि काळीं साधी कार्यासी ॥ भाकें गोंविलें विठ्ठ-
लासी ॥ ह्मणे येतों संगेसी पैं तुझ्या ॥ ३ ॥ आणीक देत वरदान ॥
तुझे वंशीं अवतरण ॥ मीस्वयें करीन आपण ॥ करीत जन उद्धार
॥ ४ ॥ आश्वासूनि भानुदास ॥ ह्मणे स्वस्थ जावें बिऱ्हाडास ॥ उदईक
होईल विलास ॥ तो सावकाश लक्षावा ॥ ५ ॥ आवडीच्या सौरसीं ॥
निज कंठींच्या माळेसी ॥ प्रसाद भानुदासासी ॥ घालून गळ्यासी बोळ-
विलें ॥ ६ ॥ पुष्प तुळसी हारातें ॥ रत्नमाळा गळां येत ॥ भानुदासा
नसे विदित ॥ स्वयें जात निजानंदें ॥ ७ ॥ उरली रात्र क्रमिल्यावरी ॥
उषःकाळीं नदी तिरीं ॥ विणा घालूनि खांद्यावरीं ॥ स्वानंदें करी कीर्तन
॥ ८ ॥ येरीकडे कांकड आरती ॥ करावया बडवे येती ॥ निर्माल्य
विसर्जितां माळेप्रती ॥ गळां न देखती देवाच्या ॥ ९ ॥ देवाचा नव-
रत्न हार ॥ चोरी गेला हें उत्तर ॥ राजा ऐकोनि चिंतातुर ॥ होऊनि
सत्वर बोलिला ॥ ११० ॥ समस्त सेवकजनीं आतां ॥ शोध कीजे
अति सत्वरता ॥ रत्नहार द्यावा तत्वतां ॥ तरीच सेवकता उपयोगी

॥ ११ ॥ ऐकतां निग्रह राजवाणी ॥ सेवक निघाले गवेषणी ॥ नगरीं आणि बाह्य स्थानीं ॥ धांवले सत्वर सज्जुनी हत्यारें ॥ १२ ॥ तव नदीतिरीं भानुदास ॥ हरिभजनीं अति उल्हास ॥ सुखें बैसला सावकाश ॥ गळां माळेस पाहिलें ॥ १३ ॥ संतोषमानुनी सेवकजन ॥ रत्नमाळा घेती हिरोन ॥ चोराचें समूळ लक्षण ॥ केलें निवेदन भूपतीसी ॥ १४ ॥ अविवेक बुद्धि राजयासी ॥ कांहीं न पुसतां शोधासी ॥ सुळीं द्यावें चोरासी ॥ या आज्ञेसी बोलिला ॥ १५ ॥ ईश्वरमायेचें कैवाड ॥ म्हणोनि बुद्धि जाली जड ॥ जिवीं संपत्तीची चाड ॥ म्हणोनि हे द्वाड जल्पला ॥ १६ ॥ सुळीं द्यावया चोर ॥ भानुदासासी धरिती हेर ॥ येरू मनीं निर्विकार ॥ शंका अणुमात्र न करीच ॥ १७ ॥ सुळा जवळीं नेऊन त्यासी ॥ म्हणती आठवावें देवासी ॥ ते काळीं अभंगासी ॥ अति उल्हासीं बोलिले ॥ १८ ॥ अभंग ॥ आकाशवरी पडों पाहे ॥ ब्रह्मगोळ भंगा जाय ॥ वडवानळ त्रिभुवन खाय ॥ तरि मी तुझीच वाट पाहें विठोबा ॥ १ ॥ आणिकाचा न करीं पांगिला ॥ नामधारक तुझाची अंकेला ॥ धृ० ॥ सप्तहि सागर समरस होती ॥ तैं हे विरोनि जाय क्षिती ॥ पंचमहाभूतें प्रळय पावती ॥ तैं तूंचि सांगाती विठोबा ॥ २ ॥ भलतेंसें जड पडो भारी ॥ परि नाम न सांडी न टळे निर्धारी ॥ पतिव्रता जेंवि प्राणेश्वरी ॥ देवा भानुदास म्हणें निर्धारी गा विठोबा ॥ ३ ॥ ओवी ॥ अभंग ऐकतां सकळां ॥ पल्लव फुटला तया शूळा ॥ देखतांचि नवललीळा ॥ केलें नृपाळा निवेदन ॥ १९ ॥ ऐकोनि दूतांची वाणी ॥ राजा आश्चर्य करी मनीं ॥ म्हणे ऐसी अघटित करणी ॥ भक्तावांचोनि कोणाची ॥ १२० ॥ चोर नव्हे तो पूर्णभक्त ॥ आतां व्हावें शरणागत ॥ पुसोनि त्याचें मनोगत ॥ पुरवूं आर्त पैं त्याचें ॥ २१ ॥ उठोनि सत्वर निजगती ॥ अनवाणी धांवे नृपती ॥ अनुतापयुक्त काकुळती ॥ येऊन करीत दंडवत ॥ २२ ॥ कोण कोठील स्वामिराया ॥ कोठोनि आलासी या ठायां ॥ अचाट दाविली हे क्रिया ॥ कोणे

कार्या कारणें ॥ २३ ॥ मीं तव अपराधी पतित ॥ येवढें आचरलों दुरित ॥ दीनदयाळू तुम्ही संत ॥ शरणांगत मीं आलों ॥ २४ ॥ भानुदास माझें नाम ॥ पंढरीहून आलों आपण ॥ देवदर्शना भाव धरून ॥ केल्या हें चिन्ह प्रगटलें ॥ २५ ॥ पंढरीस न्यावा देव ॥ हा माझा पूर्वभाव ॥ थोरथोर महानुभाव ॥ यात्रा सर्व मिळाली ॥ २६ ॥ समस्तीं मज आज्ञापून ॥ पाठवावयाचें हेंच कारण ॥ ऐकतांचि नृपतिप्राण ॥ देहांतून जाऊं पाहे ॥ २७ ॥ विव्हळित झालें मन ॥ आक्रंदें करी रूदन ॥ व्यर्थ श्रम झाले भाउन ॥ अति उद्विग्न पैं जाला ॥ २८ ॥ भानुदासासी लोटांगण ॥ घालूनि करुणा विज्ञापन ॥ ह्मणें इतुकी गोष्टी करूनि भिन्न ॥ सर्व राज्य देईन हें ॥ २९ ॥ भानुदास ऐकोनि वाणी ॥ म्हणती हे देवाची करणी ॥ कैंचें सामर्थ्य कल्पना मनीं ॥ मजलागुनी न करवे ॥ १३० ॥ जैसें देवाचें मनोगत ॥ तैसीच वर्त्तणुक होत ॥ इतुकें बोलोनि निवांत ॥ तंव राजा विनवित मागुती ॥ ३१ ॥ घालूनि लोटांगण ॥ घ्यावें आतां देवदर्शन ॥ प्रासादीं सन्मानें नेऊन ॥ मूर्त्तीचें ध्यान पाहताती ॥ ३२ ॥ म्लान वदन कलाहीन ॥ जळें वाहती लोचन ॥ स्वयें देखोनि दुश्चिन्ह ॥ मूर्च्छित जाण पडियेला ॥ ३३ ॥ म्हणे कटकटा उफराटे ॥ अदृष्ट झालें पैं खोटें ॥ देव रुसला हें मोठें ॥ दुःखें फुटे जिव्हार ॥ ३४ ॥ ऐसिये अवस्थे आंत ॥ शब्द ऐके अकस्मात ॥ मज ठेवितां निग्रह येथ ॥ पावसी अनर्थ रोकडा ॥ ३५ ॥ मनीं म्हणें येकाळीं देव ॥ निजस्थाना जावया स्वयमेव ॥ इतुकें रचितसे लाघव ॥ फिरलें दैव पैं माझें ॥ ३६ ॥ निश्चय देखोनी देवाचा ॥ राजा बोलतसे वाचा ॥ सोवळ्यानें आणिला साचा ॥ तैसाचि न्यावयाचा असे नेम ॥ ३७ ॥ परिसोनि राजयाचें वचन ॥ भानुदास बोलतसे खूण ॥ आठवून वाचाऋण ॥ व्हावें लहान ये काळीं ॥ ३८ ॥ आपण करूनि स्नान ॥ नेसूनि सोंवळें वसन ॥ देवासन्निध होऊन ॥ उचलित जाण निज करें ॥ ३९ ॥ तंव विती प्रमाण मूर्ती ॥ झाली ते काळीं

आकृती ॥ नवल देखतसे नृपती ॥ आश्चर्य चित्तीं चमत्कारला ॥ १४०
भावें धन्य भानुदास ॥ सकळ पाहती हा विलास ॥ खांदीं वाहून देवास ॥ नमून नृपतीस चालिला ॥ ४१ ॥ कोठें न राहून स्थीर ॥ अहर्निशीं निरंतर ॥ पंथ क्रमूनि सत्वर ॥ गोपाळपुर पावला ॥ ४२ ॥ हर्षे निर्भर निजमानस ॥ देखोनिया पंढरीस ॥ लोटांगण सावकाश ॥ घालीत उल्हास हृदयकमळीं ॥ ४३ ॥ देव लाघवी विचित्र ॥ कैसें केलें चरित्र ॥ भानुदास भक्त पवित्र ॥ येत सत्वर पंढरीये ॥ ४४ ॥ प्रसन्न वदन पाहून त्यासी ॥ अति उल्हास सर्वत्रांसी ॥ ज्ञानेश्वरादि महंतांसी ॥ लोटांगणेसी वंदिलें ॥ ४५ ॥ जालिया वृत्तांताचें कथन ॥ समस्त संतांसीं देखून ॥ केलें तेणें धन्य धन्य ॥ वंदोनि आलिंगन दिधलें ॥ ४६ ॥ जयजयकाराची ध्वनी ॥ नाद न माये गगनीं ॥ मंगळवाद्यें मिरवुनी ॥ विठ्ठल स्वस्थानीं स्थापिला ॥ ४७ ॥ तोचि हा पंढरिनाथ ॥ अद्यापि उभा असे समर्थ ॥ स्वामीचा प्रपितामह येथ ॥ स्वकरें स्थापित देवासी ॥ ४८ ॥ हा इतिहास पुरातन ॥ श्रीनाथांसी निवेदुन ॥ समस्तीं वंदुनी चरण ॥ वानितां महिमान निजमुखें ॥ ४९ ॥ आतां चतुर्दशीचें कीर्त्तन ॥ श्रीवदनीचें निरोपण ॥ श्रवणें करावें पावन ॥ आज्ञा वचन देवाचें ॥ १५० ॥ येथुनी चतुर्दशीचे दिवशीं ॥ कथा समर्थाची या नेमास ॥ पांडुरंगाचा विलास ॥ मान्य सर्वांस पैं जाला ॥ ५१ ॥ नाथें आलिंगुनी समस्तां ॥ ह्मणे धन्य धन्य तुमची आस्था ॥ या दिवसाचिया वृत्तांता ॥ साकल्य आचरितां ऐकविलें ॥ ५२ ॥ प्रसंगें आमुच्या पूर्वजांचें ॥ वर्तमान होतें साचें ॥ ऐकवूनि प्रेम तयाचें ॥ केलें मनाचें समाधान ॥ ५३ ॥

Appendix IV

परिशिष्ट ४

भानुदास भक्तलीलामृत

अध्याय १८

तंव कोणी प्रश्न करिती त्यांस ॥ तुमचा पूर्वज भानुदास ॥ त्याचें चरित्र अति सुरस ॥ गावोनि आह्मांस ऐकवा ॥ ७४ ॥ ऐसा श्रोतयांचा प्रश्न ऐकोनी ॥ श्रीनाथ संतोषले मनीं ॥ ह्मणती हेंचि होतें आमुचे मनीं ॥ त्यावरी स्वामीनीं आज्ञापिलें ॥ ७५ ॥ रामराजा विद्यानगरीं- ॥ परिवारेंसी राज्यकरी ॥ तो एके दिवसीं करोनि स्वारी ॥ क्षेत्र पंढरी पावला ॥ ७६ ॥ श्रीपांडुरंगमूर्ति पाहोनि सुंदर ॥ चित्तीं आवड बैसली फार ॥ ह्मणे आपुलें गांव विद्यानगर ॥ रुक्मिणीवर तेथें न्यावा ॥ ७७ ॥ ऐसी कल्पना आणोनि मानसीं ॥ सात दिवस बैसले उपवासी ॥ तंव स्वप्नीं येऊनि ह्रषीकेशी ॥ आज्ञा तयासी करिते ॥ ७८ ॥ आह्मीं पुंडलीकाची भाक्ति विशेष ॥ देखोनि पंढरीस केला वास ॥ भाकवचन देऊनि त्यास ॥ भाविकजनांस भेटतसों ॥७९॥ ये स्थळीं चित्त रमतसे ॥ ऐसी विश्रांति कोठें नसे ॥ क्षीरसागरीं आमुचा वास ॥ वैकुंठही दिसे उणेंची ॥ ८० ॥ येथें भाविक भक्त प्रेमळ ॥ यात्रेसि येती सर्वकाळ ॥ त्यांच्या संगतीनें मी घननीळ ॥ सांडोनि तळमळ राहिलों ॥ ८१ ॥ ऐसें असतां रामराया ॥ तुवां निग्रह मांडिला वायां ॥ आतां विद्यानगरासि न्यावया ॥ सांगतों उपाया त्याकरीं ॥ ८२ ॥ शुचिर्भूत सोंवळे होऊन ॥ ब्राह्मणीं उचलावें मजलागुन ॥ मार्गावरी खालीं न ठेवणें ॥ तरीच येईन त्या ठायां ॥ ८३ ॥ ऐसें स्वप्न देखतां रातीं ॥ राजा परम हर्षला

चित्तीं ॥ मग प्रधानासि पुसे एकांतीं ॥ आतां युक्ति कोणती करूं सांग ॥ ८४ ॥ मंत्री देतसे प्रतिउत्तर ॥ आपुले देशींचे द्विजवर ॥ तयांसि दक्षिणा देऊनि फार ॥ मार्गावर आणावे ॥ ८५ ॥ हातोहातीं उचलोनि मूर्ती ॥ नगरासि आणूं सत्वरगती ॥ ऐसी ऐकोनि वचनोक्ती ॥ चित्तीं भूपती संतोषला ॥ ८६ ॥ गांवोगांवींचे द्विजवर ॥ तयांसि लेहूनि विनीतपत्र ॥ ब्राह्मणसमुदाय वाटेवर ॥ आणवी सत्वर नृप तेव्हां ॥ ८७ ॥ उदकअन्नाची ठायींठायीं ॥ स्वस्थता केली ते समयीं ॥ देवकार्य ह्मणोनि पाहीं ॥ संतोष जीवीं ब्राह्मणां ॥ ८८ ॥ मग देवासि घालोनि नमस्कार ॥ प्रार्थना करितसे नृपवर ॥ आतां कृपा करोनि मजवर ॥ चला सत्वर पांडुरंगा ॥ ८९ ॥ ऐसें विनवोनियां नृपती ॥ मूर्ति चालविली हातोहातीं ॥ बडवे पुजारी तळमळती ॥ परी नायके भूपती तयांचें ॥ ९० ॥ सत्ताधारी तो भूपाळ ॥ कोणाचेही न चले बळ ॥ नरनारी पाहती सकळ ॥ भरले डोळे अश्रुपातें ॥ ९१ ॥ मूर्त्ति काढितांचि नृपवर ॥ वोस दिसतसे पंढरपुर ॥ जैसें प्राणावांचूनि शरीर ॥ तैसा विचार तो झाला ॥ ९२ ॥ असो इकडे रामराय भूपती ॥ मूर्ति चालवीत हातोहातीं ॥ परम उल्हास मानोनि चित्तीं ॥ नगराप्रती तो आला ॥ ९३ ॥ मेळवूनियां वैष्णव वीर ॥ कीर्तन करीतसे नृपवर ॥ दिंड्या पताकांचे भार ॥ मंगळ तुरे लाविले ॥ ९४ ॥ पूजा अभिषेक करोनि प्रीतीं ॥ सिंहासनीं स्थापीत पांडुरंग मूर्ती ॥ महा उत्सव करीत भूपती ॥ आनंद चित्तीं न समाये ॥ ९५ ॥ वस्त्रें भूषणें देऊनि फार ॥ राये गौरविले वैष्णव वीर ॥ द्रव्य दक्षिणा वांटोनि थोर ॥ सुखी द्विजवर ते केले ॥ ९६ ॥ रत्नजडित अळंकार ॥ अमूल्य वस्त्रें मुक्ताहार ॥ लेवोनि पूजिला रुक्मिणीवर ॥ हर्षें अंतर कोंदलें ॥ ९७ ॥ मंदिरीं निद्रिस्त होता नृपती ॥ तंव स्वप्नीं सांगत पांडुरंगमूर्ती ॥ त्वां ये स्थळीं आणिलें मजप्रती ॥ तरी सांगतों रीती ते ऐका ॥ ९८ ॥ विचारूनियां न्यायनीत ॥

धर्मराज्य करावें निश्चित ॥ तुझा अन्याय होतां किंचित ॥ मग मी येथ न राहे ॥ ९९ ॥ प्रेमळ भक्त आवडती मजसी ॥ आणि त्वां निरपराधें छळिलें त्यांसी ॥ तरी मी जाईन पंढरीसी ॥ पूर्व स्थळासी आपुल्या ॥ १०० ॥ ऐसा दृष्टांत पंढरीनाथें ॥ रात्रीं दाखविला असे त्यातें ॥ राजा होऊनि भयभीत ॥ असे सावचित्त सर्वदा ॥ १ ॥ पुजारी येऊनि निजप्रीतीं ॥ प्रातःकाळीं अर्चन करिती ॥ स्नान करोनि येतसे भूपती ॥ पूजा आरती पाहातसे ॥ २ ॥ देवावरी अमूल्य अळंकार ॥ यास्तव तस्कराचें भय फार ॥ कवाडांसि कुलुपें अष्टही प्रहर ॥ होय सायंकाळ तोंवरी ॥ ३ ॥ राजा देउळीं असल्यावीण ॥ नगरवासी अवघे जण ॥ कोणासि न होय दर्शन ॥ केलें संरक्षण या रीतीं ॥ ४ ॥ षोडशोपचारें करोनि जाण ॥ राजा करितसे नित्य पूजन ॥ घृतपाचित पक्वान्नें ॥ त्रिकाळ अर्पण होतसे ॥ ५ ॥ भोंवते कापूरदीपक ॥ सर्वदा जळती सम्यक ॥ पुष्पें कस्तूरी सुवासिक ॥ उपचार अनेक वोळंगती ॥ ६ ॥ परी पंढरीच्या वियोगबाणें ॥ चैन न पडे देवाकारणें ॥ म्हणे प्राप्त जाहले बंदिखाने ॥ कधीं सुटेन येथोनियां ॥ ७ ॥ असो इकडे आषाढ मासीं ॥ यात्रा मिळाली पंढरीसी ॥ संत महंत सिद्ध ऋषी ॥ चिंता मानसीं करिताती ॥ ८ ॥ निधडे वैष्णव वारकरी निश्चित ॥ तितुके मात्र आले तेथ ॥ इतर प्रापंचीक लोक समस्त ॥ म्हणती पंढरीनाथ दूर गेला ॥ ९ ॥ ऐसें समजोनि ते अवसरीं ॥ राहती आपुलिया घरीं ॥ संत महंत यांनीं साजिरी ॥ केली पंढरी तेधवां ॥ ११० ॥ जेवीं पृथ्वीवरी मेघ वर्षतां ॥ आड वोहळांच्या भासती सरिता ॥ उष्णकाळ येतांचि तत्त्वतां ॥ बुंद आतौता न थारे ॥ ११ ॥ घणघायीं टिकतां साचार ॥ तेचि जाणावे अमूल्य हिरे ॥ इतर गारांचा होतसे चूर ॥ परीक्षक नर जाणती ॥ १२ ॥ तावोनि काढितां सोज्वळ दिसे ॥ यालागीं कांचन म्हणावें त्यास ॥ पितळेसि काळिमा चढतसे ॥ परीक्षा असे हे त्याची ॥ १३ ॥ कां मोहऱ्यांसि गुंडाळूनि सूत ॥ टाकूनि

पाहिजे अग्नी आंत ॥ तंतू न जळे तरी निश्चित ॥ विष उतरत त्याचेनी ॥ १४ ॥ तेंवी विषम काळ जाहलिया प्राप्त ॥ त्रितापांचे नाना आवर्त ॥ ज्याचा निश्चय न टळेचि सत्य ॥ तरी तोचि संत म्हणावा ॥ १५ ॥ महा संकटीं न ढळेचि प्रेमा ॥ निग्रहें चालवीत आपुल्या नेमा ॥ तो भक्त आवडे पुरुषोत्तमा ॥ जैसा जीवात्मा या रीतीं ॥ १६ ॥ असोत हीं भाषणें बहुत ॥ दृष्टांत देणें कवीचें मत ॥ रामरायें नेतां पंढरीनाथ ॥ तों पातले संत वारकरी ॥ १७ ॥ सिंहासनीं नसतां रुक्मिणीवर ॥ वोस दिसतसे पंढरपुर ॥ जैसें प्राणावांचूनि शरीर ॥ खुंटे व्यापार इंद्रियांचा ॥ १८ ॥ नृपावांचूनि सैन्य संपत्ती ॥ कां चंद्रावांचूनि जैसी राती ॥ ईश्वरकृपेनें निश्चिती ॥ कवित्वस्फूर्ती जेविं होय ॥ १९ ॥ ना तरी घरधन्यावांचूनि घर ॥ तैसें दिसे पंढरपुर ॥ चिंता करिती निरंतर ॥ परी उपाय अणुमात्र सुचेना ॥ १२० ॥ तंव निवृत्ति ज्ञानदेव सोपान ॥ नामा सांवता वैष्णव जाण ॥ मुक्ताबाई गुणनिधान ॥ यात्रेसि संपूर्ण हे आले ॥ २१ ॥ कबीर आणि रोहिदास पाहीं ॥ गोराकुंभार गोणाबायी ॥ जनी दासी नामया पाहीं ॥ आणि राजायी भक्तराज ॥ २२ ॥ इतुकी मंडळी ते अवसरीं ॥ बैसली असे गरुडपारीं ॥ नामदेव तेथें कीर्तन करी ॥ तों भानुदास सत्वरी पातले ॥ २३ ॥ खांद्यावरी घेतला ब्रह्मविणा ॥ आलापें गीत गातसे नाना ॥ हृदयीं चिंतोनि रुक्मिणीरमणा ॥ नामस्मरणा करीतसे ॥ २४ ॥ ऐशा स्थितीनें ते अवसरीं ॥ भानुदास पातले गरुडपारीं ॥ संत महंता भेटोनि सत्वरीं ॥ मग नमस्कार करिती सद्भावें ॥ २५ ॥ विद्यानगरासि रुक्मिणीवर ॥ नेला म्हणवोनि वैष्णव वीर ॥ अवघेचि होऊनि चिंतातुर ॥ करिती विचार एकमेकां ॥ २६ ॥ रामरायाचा देखोनि भाव ॥ पंढरीहूनी गेले देवाधिदेव ॥ आपण इतुके भक्त वैष्णव ॥ तरी जावोनि केशव आणावा ॥ २७ ॥ ज्ञानराज बोलतां ऐसें ॥ कोणीच उत्तर न देती त्यास ॥ म्हणती ईश्वर इच्छेस ॥ उपाय नसे आपुला ॥ २८ ॥ एक बोलती

अद्वैत भाव ॥ आपुलेच देहीं असे देव ॥ चराचरीं भरला असे सर्व ॥ याजवीण ठाव रिता नाहीं ॥ २९ ॥ एक म्हणती जातांचि तेथें ॥ नृपवर कोपेल आम्हांतें ॥ कोंडूनि ठेवील बंदिखान्यांत ॥ मग कैसी मात करावी ॥ १३० ॥ हेंचि कार्य नव्हे आमुचेनें ॥ ऐसें अधीर बोलती वचन ॥ तों भानुदास साष्टांग नमन ॥ संताकारणें करीतसे ॥ ३१ ॥ जरी आज्ञा द्याल मज आतां ॥ तरी सत्वर आणितों पंढरीनाथा ॥ तुम्ही सांडूनि सकळ चिंता ॥ या स्थळीं तत्वता आसिजे ॥ ३२ ॥ ऐसें बोलोनि तयांस ॥ तेथोनि निघे भानुदास ॥ जेवीं मारुती जातां सीताशुद्धीस ॥ तैसा उल्हास वाटला ॥ ३३ ॥ हृदयीं चिंतोनि पांडुरंगमूर्ती ॥ मुखीं गातसे नामकीर्ती ॥ स्मरण करितां दिवस रातीं ॥ सप्रेम विश्रांती सर्वदा ॥ ३४ ॥ देवासि घेऊनि येईन कवतुकें ॥ म्हणोनि चित्तीं वाटला हरिख ॥ विदेह स्थिति जाहली देख ॥ ताहान-भूख विसरला ॥ ३५ ॥ अयाचित वृत्ती करून ॥ कोणीं अकस्मात दीधलें अन्न ॥ स्वसंतोषें भक्षून ॥ पुढती गमन करितसे ॥ ३६ ॥ ऐशा रीतीं क्रमितां पंथ ॥ विद्यानगरासि भानुदास येत ॥ ये स्थळीं आणिला पंढरीनाथ ॥ ऐसें पुसत लोकांसी ॥ ३७ ॥ रायाच्या भयें करोनि जाण ॥ कोणीच न बोलती वचन ॥ तों एक सत्पुरुष भेटला ब्राह्मण ॥ तो साकल्य निवेदन करीतसे ॥ ३८ ॥ म्हणे रामरायें आणूनियां पांडुरंगमूर्ती ॥ देउळीं स्थापिली असे निश्चिती ॥ परी दर्शन नव्हेचि कोणा-प्रती ॥ कुलुपें घालिती सर्वदा ॥ ३९ ॥ मग भानुदास विचारी मनांत ॥ आपणासि पाहिजे एकांत ॥ तरी शेजआरती झालिया निश्चित ॥ जावें त्वरित त्या ठाया ॥ ४० ॥ तये दिवसीं रात्रीं निश्चित ॥ राउळासि आला नृपनाथ ॥ शेजारती करोनि त्वरित ॥ मग स्वस्थानासि जात आपल्या ॥ ४१ ॥ पुजारी असती बाहेर ॥ तेही निद्रेनें व्यापिले फार ॥ तेथें भानुदास वैष्णव वीर ॥ द्वारासमोर येत तेव्हां ॥ ४२ ॥ एकांत एक चार द्वारें ॥ तितुक्यांस कुलुपें असती थोर ॥ तों माव केली

रुक्मिणीवरें ॥ गळोणि सत्वर पडिलीं तीं ॥ ४३ ॥ कपाटें मोकळीं सर्वही ॥ भानुदासासि आनंद वाटला जीवीं ॥ म्हणे मनोरथ पुरले ये समयीं ॥ मग आंत लवलाहीं प्रवेशला ॥ ४४ ॥ तों ठाणठकारें जगजेठी ॥ समपद जोडिले विटे नेहटी ॥ दोन्ही कर ठेवूनि कटीं ॥ नासाग्रीं दृष्टी धरियेली ॥ ४५ ॥ साजिरें मुख देखतांचि नयनीं ॥ भानुदासासि उल्हास मनीं ॥ मग बात्यात्कारें राग धरोनी ॥ देवासि ते क्षणीं भांडतसे ॥ ४६ ॥ म्हणे रुक्मिणीपति पंढरीराया ॥ पायीं बिरुद बांधिलें कासया ॥ तुझी बोलण्यासारखी नसेचि क्रिया ॥ माझिया प्रत्यया हें आलें ॥ ४७ ॥ तुवां पुंडलीकासि दीधला वर ॥ कीं तेथें असावें निरंतर ॥ करावा जडमूढ उद्धार ॥ तो आठव अणुमात्र तुज नाहीं ॥ ४८ ॥ राजमंदिरीं एकांत ॥ बरा पाहोनि बैसलासि येथ ॥ वस्त्रें अळंकार ल्यालासि बहुत ॥ नैवेद्यासि मिळत पक्वान्नें ॥ ४९ ॥ यास्तव सुरवाडें राहिलासि हरी ॥ आमुचा विसर पडिला अंतरीं ॥ मग स्वमुखें अभंग केला सत्वरी ॥ तो सादर चतुरीं परिसावा ॥ १५० ॥ अभंग ॥ चंद्रभागेतीरीं उभा विटेवरी ॥ विठो राज्या करी पंढरीये ॥ १ ॥ ऋद्धिसिद्धि वोळंगती परिवार ॥ न लाहाती अवसर ब्रह्मादिकां ॥ २ ॥ सांडुनी इतुकें येथें बीजें केलें ॥ कवणें चाळविलें कानडीया ॥ ३ ॥ शंख भेरी मृदंग वाजतीकाहळा ॥ उपवड राऊळा होत असे ॥ ४ ॥ चांपेल मार्जन सुगंध चर्चन ॥ भिवरा चंदन पाट वाहे ॥ ५ ॥ रंभा तिळोत्तमा उर्वशी मेनीका ॥ कामिनी अनेका येती सवें ॥ ६ ॥ कनकाचे पयेळीं रत्नाचे दीपक ॥ सुंदर श्रीमुख वोवाळीती ॥ ७ ॥ रखुमाई आई ते जाहली उदास ॥ पुंडलीका कैसें पडिलें मौन ॥ ८ ॥ भक्त भागवत सकळ पांरूसले ॥ निःशब्दचि ठेले तुजवीण ॥ ९ ॥ धन्य पंढरपुर विश्वाचें माहेर ॥ धन्य भीमातीर वाळुवंट ॥ १० ॥ भानुदास म्हणे चाले आम्हांसवें ॥ वाचाऋण देवें आठवावें ॥ ११ ॥ ओवी ॥ ऐसी करुणा वदोनियां ॥ भानुदास

लागतसे पायां ॥ म्हणे कोणें चाळविलासि देवराया ॥ सांग लवलाह्यां ये समयीं ॥ ९१ ॥ ऐसी करुणा ऐकोनि कानीं ॥ सद्गदित जाहले चक्रपाणी ॥ भानुदासासि आलिंगुनी ॥ हृदयभुवनीं धरियेले ॥ ९२ ॥ मग काय बोलती पंढरीनाथ ॥ मी बंदिखान्यांत पडिलों येथ ॥ तुम्हींही निष्ठुर करूनि चित्त ॥ आमुची परत न केली ॥ ९३ ॥ मजला टाकोनि प्रेमळ भक्ता ॥ सर्वथा जाऊं नको आतां ॥ तुम्हांवांचोनि मज तत्त्वतां ॥ क्षणही निरुता न कंठे ॥ ९४ ॥ ऐसें म्हणोनि करुणामूर्ती ॥ भानुदासासि प्रसाद देती ॥ तुळसी सुमनांचा हार निगुती ॥ गळां घालिती तयाचे ॥ ९५ ॥ म्हणे उदईक येऊनि सत्वर ॥ मज नेयी आपुल्याबरोबर ॥ ऐसें सांगतां रुक्मिणीवर ॥ हर्ष थोर वाटला ॥ ९६ ॥ पुष्पमाळेच्याबरोबर ॥ आला नवरत्नांचाहार ॥ भानुदास नेणती साचार ॥ आले सत्वर बाहेरी ॥ ९७ ॥ मागुतीं लाघवी जगज्जीवन ॥ कवाडकुलुपांसि केलें बंधन ॥ प्रातःकाळ होतांचि-त्वरेनें ॥ नृपनंदन पातला ॥ ९८ ॥ कांकडआरती करितां साचार ॥ तों कंठीं न दिसे नवरत्नहार ॥ म्हणती येथें कोण आला चोर ॥ कोपे नृपवर पुजाऱ्यासी ॥ ९९ ॥ तस्कर पाहावयासि साचार ॥ अष्टदिशा धांवले हेर ॥ तों भानुदास वैष्णव वीर ॥ त्यांणीं सत्वर देखिला ॥ १६० ॥ गंगातीरीं करोनि स्नान ॥ करीत बैसला विठ्ठल-स्मरण ॥ कंठीं झळकती दिव्यरत्नें ॥ सेवकजन देखती ॥ ६१ ॥ त्यांणीं धरोनि वैष्णव वीर ॥ रायापासीं आणिला सत्वर ॥ म्हणती धरोनि आणिला चोर ॥ रत्नहार दाखविला ॥ ६२ ॥ चित्तीं क्षोभला नृपवर ॥ सक्रोध बोले तयासि उत्तर ॥ धरोनि आणिला आहे तस्कर ॥ तरी सुळावर त्यासि घाला ॥ ६३ ॥ विवेक नीत न विचारून ॥ सेवकांसि आज्ञा केली त्याणें ॥ होणार भविष्य सर्वथा नेणें ॥ मायाभ्रांतीनें वेष्टिला ॥ ६४ ॥ असो भानुदास वैष्णव वीर ॥ तयासि दंड केला फार ॥ सूळ देऊनि खांद्यावर ॥ माथां सेंदुर घातला ॥ ६५ ॥

भानुदास प्रेम चित्तीं हृदयीं चिंतिली पांडुरंगमूर्ती ॥ म्हणे देवाधिदेवा रुक्मिणीपती ॥ उत्तम युक्ती त्वां केली ॥ ६६ ॥ तुज न्यावयासि आलों साचार ॥ यास्तव गळां घातला हार ॥ आतां देववितोसि सुळावर ॥ माया अणुमात्र ॥ तुज नाहीं ॥ ६७ ॥ आतां जैसें चित्तीं असेल जाण ॥ तैसेंचि देहासि येईल मरण ॥ परी सर्वथा न सोडीं तुझें स्मरण ॥ मग स्वमुखें वचन बोलिले ॥ ६८ ॥ अभंग ॥ आकाश कडकडोनियां पाहे ॥ कीं ब्रह्मगोळ भंगला जाय ॥ वडवानळ त्रिभुवन खाय ॥ तैं तुझी वाट पाहे विठोबा ॥ १ ॥ सप्तही समुद्र समरस होती ॥ लय पावेल हे क्षिती ॥ पंचभूतें प्रळय पावती ॥ तैं तूं माझा सांगाती विठोबा ॥ २ ॥ भलतैसें पडो भारी ॥ नामा न टळों निर्धारी ॥ पतिव्रता प्राणेश्वरी ॥ भानुदास म्हणे अवधारी विठोबा ॥ ३ ॥ ओव्या ॥ ऐसा निश्चय करोनि तेथें ॥ कंठ जाहला सद्गदित ॥ तों तयासि पावले पंढरीनाथ ॥ तें ऐका निजभक्त भाविक हो ॥ १६९ ॥ सूळ रोविला होता जेथ ॥ त्यासि पल्लव शाखा फुटल्या बहुत ॥ पुष्पीं फळीं सुशोभित ॥ आश्चर्य वाटत सकळांसी ॥ १७० ॥ सूळ वृक्ष झाला म्हणवून ॥ रायासि सांगती सेवकजन ॥ ऐसें ऐकतांचि वचन ॥ नृपनंदन दचकला ॥ ७१ ॥ राजा अनुताप धरोनियां ॥ सत्वर चालिला पाहावया ॥ तों भानुदास नेत्र झांकोनियां ॥ पंढरीराया आठवित ॥ ७२ ॥ ऐसें देखोनि नृपवर ॥ घालीत साष्टांग नमस्कार ॥ म्हणे तूं निधडा वैष्णव वीर ॥ मी नेणेंचि पामर मूढमती ॥ ७३ ॥ भानुदास पाहे उघडोनि नेत्र ॥ तों सूळाचा वृक्ष जाहला थोर ॥ म्हणे मज पावला रुक्मिणीवर ॥ अघटित विचार हा झाला ॥ ७४ ॥ भानुदासासि धरोनि हातीं ॥ राउळासि घेऊनि येत भूपती ॥ तों म्लानमुख पांडुरंग-मूर्ती ॥ अश्रु वाहती नेत्रांतुनी ॥ ७५ ॥ ऐसें देखोनि नृपवर ॥ घातला साष्टांग नमस्कार ॥ हात जोडोनि देवासमोर ॥ मधुरोत्तरें विनवीतसे ॥ ७६ ॥ म्हणे मी अपराधी नाना ॥ तुझ्या भक्ताची केली छळणा ॥ रामरायाची ऐकूनि करुणा ॥ पंढरीराणा काय वदे ॥ ७७ ॥

आतां माझेंरूप आठवूनि अंतरीं ॥ सुखें राहावें आपुले नगरीं ॥ आम्ही भानुदासाच्या बरोबरी ॥ जातों पंढरी पाहावया ॥ ७८ ॥ यावरी आग्रह करिसील जर ॥ तरी अनर्थ येथें होईल थोर ॥ ऐसें वदतां शार्ङ्गधर ॥ निवांत नृपवर राहिला ॥ ७९ ॥ भानुदास म्हणे रुक्मिणी-कांता ॥ कैसा उपाय करावा आतां ॥ माझी तों नाहीं राजसत्ता ॥ मी मेळवूनि बहुतां तुज नेऊं ॥ १८० ॥ ऐसी ऐकूनि वचनोक्ती ॥ लाघव करीत रुक्मिणीपती ॥ तत्काळ लहान जाहली मूर्ती ॥ विस्मित चित्तीं नृपनाथ ॥ ८१ ॥ भानुदास संतोष पावूनि मना ॥ संबळींत घातला पंढरीराणा ॥ जय श्रीविठ्ठल बोलोनि वचन ॥ रुक्मिणीरमणा उचलिलें ॥ ८२ ॥ संबळीआडोनि जगजेठी ॥ भानुदासासीं बोले गुजगोष्टी ॥ आज परमानंदें भरिलीसृष्टी ॥ होतील भेटी संतांच्या ॥ ८३ ॥ ऐशा रीतीं क्रमितां पंथ ॥ भानुदास आले पंढरीसि त्वरित ॥ पद्मतीर्थीं वैष्णव भक्त ॥ उतरे स्नानार्थ ते समयीं ॥ ८४ ॥ धोत्रें धुवोनि ते वेळीं ॥ वाळूं घालीत सरोवर पाळीं ॥ संबळींत होते वनमाळी ॥ ते थोर तत्काळीं वाढले ॥ ८५ ॥ वरील पूड मस्तकावरी ॥ तळीचें पायीं जाहलें चुरी ॥ भानुदास विस्मित अंतरीं ॥ मग रुक्मिणीवर काय म्हणे ॥ ८६ ॥ संत महंत गरुडपारीं ॥ वाट पाहाती निरंतरी ॥ तयां जाऊनि सांग सत्वरी ॥ येतील सामोरी मज आतां ॥ ८७ ॥ ऐसें सांगतां जगज्जीवन ॥ भानुदास संतोषला मनें ॥ गरुडपारीं सत्वर येऊन ॥ हास्यवदन बोलत ॥ ८८ ॥ पद्मतीर्थ विठ्ठलमूर्ती ॥ घेऊनि आलों मी निश्चितीं ॥ ऐसी ऐकतांचि वचनोक्ती ॥ उल्हास चित्तीं सकळांच्या ॥ ८९ ॥ शिबिका घेऊनि सत्वर ॥ सकळ चालिले सामोरे ॥ दिंड्यापताकांचे भार ॥ मंगळ तुरे वाजती ॥ १९० ॥ वैष्णव करिती हरिकीर्त्तन ॥ गाती नाचती प्रीतीकरून ॥ क्षेत्रवासी सकळ जन ॥ थोर लहान चालिले ॥ ९१ ॥ म्हणती भानुदासाचा उपकार ॥ आम्हीं फेडावा कोठवर ॥ धन्य हा निधडा वैष्णववीर ॥

सारंगधर आणिला ॥ ९२ ॥ सकळ मंडळीसहित निश्चिती ॥ पद्मतीर्थी चालत येती ॥ दृष्टीसि देखूनि पांडुरंगमूर्ती ॥ सप्रेम घालिती दंडवत ॥ ९३ ॥ भानुदासानें लावूनि हात ॥ शिबिकेंत घातला पंढरीनाथ ॥ जयजयकारें गर्जती भक्त ॥ बुका उधळित निजहस्तें ॥ ९४ ॥ ऐसा मिरवत रुक्मिणीपती ॥ चंद्रभागेसि तेव्हां आणिती ॥ स्नान घालोनि सत्वरगती ॥ देऊळाप्रती मग येत ॥ ९५ ॥ सुदिन मुहूर्त तये दिनीं ॥ मूर्ति स्थापिली सिंहासनीं ॥ तंव भानुदासासि कैवल्यदानीं ॥ वरद वाणी बोलत ॥ ९६ ॥ न फिटेचि तुझा उपकार ॥ दृष्टीसि दाविलें पंढरपुर ॥ मी तुझे वंशीं अवतार ॥ घेईन साचार निश्चिती ॥ ९७ ॥ ऐसें वदतां जगदुद्धार ॥ भक्त गर्जती जयजयकार ॥ क्षेत्रवासी नारीनर ॥ आनंद थोर त्यांसि जाहला ॥ ९८ ॥ अवर्षणीं पडला जैसा घन ॥ कां शरीरांत आला मरणीं प्राण ॥ तैसा उत्सव मानोनि मनें ॥ लोक संतर्पण करिती ॥ ९९ ॥ आपुलाल्या मतें नरनारी ॥ साकरा वांटिती घरोघरीं ॥ वैष्णव येऊनि गरुडपारीं ॥ कीर्तनगजरीं डुल्लती ॥ २०० ॥ यापरी भानुदास आख्यान ॥ गातसे एका जनार्दन ॥ संत महंत ऐकोनि कीर्तन ॥ तटस्थ होऊन राहिले ॥ १ ॥ आपला पूर्वज भानुदास ॥ त्याचें चरित्र गायिलें सुरस ॥ नादब्रह्मचि आलें मुसें ॥ कीर्तनीं धोष करिताती ॥ २ ॥ मग उजळोनि मंगळ आरती ॥ वोवाळिला श्रीरुक्मिणीपती ॥ तेथें दासानुदास महीपती ॥ खिरापती वांटितसे ॥ ३ ॥ स्वस्ति श्रीभक्तलीलामृत ग्रंथ ॥ श्रवणेंचि पुरती मनोरथ ॥ प्रेमळ परिसोत भाविक भक्त ॥ अष्टादशाध्याय रसाळ हा ॥ २०४ ॥

अध्याय १८, अभंग २, ओव्या २०४.

Appendix V

परिशिष्ट ५.

शिरगांवकर भीमस्वामीकृत भानुदासचरित्र.

॥ **श्रीराम** ॥ भानुदास स्वामी संतांमाजीं श्रेष्ठ । प्रपंचाचे कष्ट दूर जया ॥ १ ॥ कापड आणाया गेलें संग्यासवें । अद्भुताचि देवें केलें तेथें ॥ २ ॥ खेप भरोनीया येतां मार्गावरी । पालें दिल्हीं बरीं गांवापासीं ॥ ३ ॥ यांचें पाल मध्यें होतें हे गांवांत । कीर्तनासी जात ऐकावया ॥ ४ ॥ सर्वांनीं वर्जीलें परी न राहीले । स्मरणीं रंगले देवाजीचे ॥ ५ ॥ रित्या पेंवामध्यें दीड पालें यांचीं । टाकतां तयांची बुद्धि ऐसी ॥ ६ ॥ बैल सारे रानीं दिधले हांकोनी । रडऊं तया मनीं भावना हे ॥ ७ ॥ चोर आले धाडी मोठी अकस्मात । लुटोनीया नेत सर्व यांचें ॥ ८ ॥ भानुदास आले कीर्तन ऐकोनी । पाहाती नयनीं जाहालें तें ॥ ९ ॥ माझें सर्व देवा केलेंसी जतन । परी संगी जाण माझे कीं हे ॥ १० ॥ तेव्हां पांडुरंगें चोर अंध केले । प्रातःकाळीं आले घेवोनीया ॥ ११ ॥ ज्याचें त्यासी दिल्हें आनंद जाहाला । वाटीलें द्विजाला आपुलें जें ॥ १२ ॥ सोडोनीया वेवसाव विणा हातीं । भजनीं रंगती अहिर्निसीं ॥ १३ ॥ संताचें चरित्र गातां आणि ऐकतां । होय सार्थकता भीम ह्मणे ॥ १४ ॥

॥ **श्रीराम** ॥ घरीं आले बहु दरिद्रें पिडीलें । कांता तेव्हां बोले दीनरूपें ॥ १ ॥ प्रातःकाळीं गंगास्नान करोनीया । गीतापाठी तया प्रीति फार ॥ २ ॥ योगक्षेम त्यांचा वाहातों मी ऐसें । अनन्य विश्वासें भजती जे ॥ ३ ॥ लोक पाहोनीया विस्मित जाहाले । द्वारताळें लावीलें तयालागीं ॥ ४ ॥ देव घरीं आले माल घेवोनीया । कांता

पुसे तया कोण तुह्मी ॥ ५ ॥ कृष्णाजीपंत हे नाम सांगीतलें । द्रव्यें अन्न केलें तृप्त तये ॥ ६ ॥ जन्मवरी खातां न सरेचि ऐसें । देवोनी विश्वासें बोलीयले ॥ ७ ॥ तुमच्या भ्रतारासी निरोप सांगावा । दृढ धरुनी जीवामाजीं ऐका ॥ ८ ॥ आमुचे दाढीं त्यांनीं लाविली हार्ताळ । पुसानी तात्काळ टाका सांग ॥ ९ ॥ इतुकें सांगोनीया गेले तों हे आले । घरीं जों पाहीलें अद्भुतचि ॥ १० ॥ पुसतां कांतेसी सांगे वर्तमान । नेत्रीं वाहाती जाण अश्रुधारा ॥ ११ ॥ तात्काळ हार्ताळ पुसोन टाकिली । भक्तासी सांभाळी हेचि सत्य ॥ १२ ॥ कांतेसी म्हणती सर्वस्वाचें दान । करावेंसें जाण वाटताहे ॥ १३ ॥ बोलावोनी विप्र फडशा केला सारा । म्हणे ज्याचें त्याला समर्पिलें ॥ १४ ॥ ऐसें हरिभक्त उदास मानसीं । देव तयापासी भीम ह्मणे ॥ १५ ॥

श्रीराम ॥ भानुदास क्षेत्र पैठणाहूनीया । पंढरी जावया सिद्ध जाले ॥ १ ॥ आले पंढरीस नेम यांचा असे । प्रेमाच्या उल्हासें गावें भावें ॥ २ ॥ देवापुढें पांच अभंग ह्मणावे । देवें माळ द्यावें अकस्मात ॥ ३ ॥ येका शिष्यें यांसी पितांबर दिला । आले राउळाला नित्या ऐसे ॥ ४ ॥ तेथें होता सडा चिडचिडीत जालें । पितांबरामुळें काय केलें ॥ ५ ॥ राखोनी नमन केलें वरिच्यावरी । तये अवसरीं माळ न ये ॥ ६ ॥ बहुत श्रम जाले न ये माळ जेव्हां । उपेक्षीलें तेव्हां ह्मणती देवें ॥ ७ ॥ तेथोनी निघाले येका गांवा आले । लोकांसी बोलीले तेथीलीया ॥ ८ ॥ प्रहररात्रीसी विघ्न येईल येथें । मारोनी तयातें टाका तुह्मी ॥ ९ ॥ पंढरीहून ते होते दोन कोस । ह्मणती जीवा नाश करूं आतां ॥ १० ॥ चौघे गडी केलें तयांसी ह्मणती । माझिये मोटेसी बांधोनी न्या ॥ ११ ॥ तया गांवांमध्यें नेवोनी ठेवावें । मग तुह्मीं यावें पंढरीस ॥ १२ ॥ आज्ञा ह्मणोनीया नेली मोट गांवीं । ठेविली जाणावी गांवांमध्यें ॥ १३ ॥ निघोनीया गडी गेल्यावरी लोक । मार करिती देख तयांवरी ॥ १४ ॥ बहु केला मार परी न लागेचि ।

मागें प्रल्हादाची साक्ष यांसी ॥ १५ ॥ धीट गेले मोटे सोडोनी पाहीले । स्वामींस देखीलें अकस्मात ॥ १६ ॥ नमन करिती पायांस लागती । तेथोनीया येती पंढरीस ॥ १७ ॥ निग्रह करीतां ह्मणे पांडुरंग । सोवळ्याचें मग स्मरण दिल्हें ॥ १८ ॥ समाधान केलें माळेसी दीधलें । पैठणासी आले आनंदानें ॥ १९ ॥ पुढील चरित्र.विस्तार बहुत । भीम गाय नित्य संतलीला ॥ २० ॥

॥ **श्रीराम** ॥ अनेगोंदीमध्यें होता नृपनाथ । कानडा विख्यात रामराजा ॥ १ ॥ रासाईचा भक्त होता तो अत्यंत । साक्षात्कार सत्य होता मोठा ॥ २ ॥ अभिमान तया जाहाला अत्यंत । वैभवी आणि भक्त मीच ह्मणे ॥ ३ ॥ हेमाडपंतही तेथें होतें जाण । त्यांसी गजानन साह्य सदा ॥ ४ ॥ लंके बिभीषणें नेलें होतें ज्यासी पिशाच्चलिपीसी आणिलें ज्यांनीं ॥ ५ ॥ रायापासीं येतां बोलिला अभिमानें । आम्हां ऐसा कोण भक्त बोला ॥ ६ ॥ वैभवही थोर भक्तही मी थोर । देवी माझी थोर सर्वांमध्यें ॥ ७ ॥ हेमाडपंतांसी न सांवरे जेव्हां । बोलीयले तेव्हां निशकचि ॥ ८ ॥ पंढरींत पांडुरंग देव येक । ऐसा नाहीं देख भूमंडळीं ॥ ९ ॥ तयाचाचि भक्त नामदेव संत । वैभव अद्भुत तेथें आहे ॥ १० ॥ रायासी आवेश येवोनी निघाला । सर्व वैभवाला घेवोनीया ॥ ११ ॥ यांनीं करोनीया गणपतीच्या ध्याना । ह्मणती माझ्या वचना सांभाळावें ॥ १२ ॥ अभय होताचि चालीयले मार्गीं । सेना दोहीं भागीं चतुरंग ॥ १३ ॥ आठ कोसांवरी राहिली पंढरी । भक्तसाहे करी पांडुरंग ॥ १४ ॥ अतद्भुचि माव करी तो देवाजी । द्वारकाचि दुजी ऐसे भासे ॥ १५ ॥ घोड्यावरी स्वार होवोनी आपण । आले नारायण रायापुढें ॥ १६ ॥ रायें पाहातांचि ह्मणे नामदेव । नमन सद्भावें करुनी पुसे ॥ १७ ॥ कृष्णाजीपंत हें नाम जाणवीलें । नामदेवें केलें पांगे आह्मां ॥ १८ ॥ सांगोनीया जातां म्हणतसे राव । धन्य हें वैभव वाटतसें ॥ १९ ॥ भुलोनीया आम्ही

पाग्याच्या पायांसी । लागलों हे ऐसी भ्रांति जाली ॥ २० ॥ ऐसीं बहु
सांगें पांडुरंग दावी । न धरवे जीवीं ब्रम्हादिकां ॥ २१ ॥ पंढरी येवोनी
पाहाताती तंव । कळस कोट सर्व सुवर्णाचे ॥ २२ ॥ हेमाडपंतांसी
घेवोनी वाड्यांत । रत्नें वस्त्रें घेत अमोलिक ॥ २३ ॥ येतां कचेरींत
बैसले लोडासी । नामदेव त्यांसी मानीयले ॥ २४ ॥ नमन करोनी
वस्त्रें रत्नें दिल्हीं । आलिंगनें जालीं पुढें ऐका ॥ २५ ॥ राव म्हणे
नाम सांगावें आपुलें । नारायण भले म्हणती आम्हां ॥ २६ ॥ नाम-
देवाचीये असो कोठीवरी । त्यांचा आम्हांवरी लोभ फार ॥ २७ ॥
तुम्ही सर्व आजि यावें भोजनासी । मग भेटी त्यासी करूं तुम्हां ॥ २८ ॥
अधिकारासारीखे बैसवीले पाहा । आली वाढावया जगन्माता ॥ २९ ॥
नामदेवाची हे पत्नी म्हणऊन । राव तये नमन करीताहे ॥ ३० ॥
पुसतां सांगती नारोपंतकांता । कोठीवरी होता तयाची हे ॥ ३१ ॥
हेमाडपंतांसी म्हणे राव काय । वैभव हें आहे न वर्णवे ॥ ३२ ॥
ऐकतांचि यांच्या नेत्रीं आले अश्रु । म्हणती सर्वेश्वरु जाला सारें ॥ ३३ ॥
भोजन करोनी चंद्रभागेतीरीं । पाहाताती नेत्री कौतुकासी ॥ ३४ ॥
शतावधि दासी भांडीं घांसितासी । विजे ऐशा दिसती राजयासी ॥ ३५ ॥
रासाईही त्यांत होती वोळखोन । साष्टांग नमन करी तये ॥ ३६ ॥
म्हणे माते ऐसें काय हें करीसी । सांग निश्चयेंसीं आजि मज ॥ ३७ ॥
म्हणे देवी तुझा देव आहे तेथें । चाकरीचें नातें येथें आहे ॥ ३८ ॥
विस्मये होवोनी म्हणे दासीपण । सोडवीन जाण चिंता नाहीं ॥ ३९ ॥
नामदेवाचीये भेटीसी चालीला । राउळांत आला देवाचिये ॥ ४० ॥
खांद्यावरी वीणा डोईस बोडके । पांई चाळ निके बांधीयले ॥ ४१ ॥
गांडींत लंगोटी भजनीं रंगले । रायानें देखीले अकस्मात ॥ ४२ ॥
रायासी सांगती हेचि नामदेव । ऐकतां सद्भाव जाला मोठा ॥ ४३ ॥
संतदर्शनाचा माहिमा अद्भुत । राव दंडवत पडे पांई ॥ ४४ ॥
उठवोनी यांनीं आलिंगन दिल्हें । प्रेमें गहिंवरले नेत्र तेव्हां ॥ ४५ ॥

म्हणे राव रासाईस मुक्त करा । देव माझा खरा आहे जी हा ॥ ४६ ॥
नामदेव म्हणती दासीपण आहे । देवपण पाहें तंवरीच ॥ ४७ ॥
सरकरांतुनीया दूर केल्यावर । सत्ता तिळमात्र न चालेचि ॥ ४८ ॥
मनामध्यें राव बहु संकोचला । दासीलागीं केला देव आम्हीं ॥ ४९ ॥
इचा देव धनी कोण तोचि पाहूं । तयालागीं वाहूं जीवप्राण ॥ ५० ॥
आला देवाल्यांत पांडुरंगापुढें । निग्रहासी गाढें आरंभीलें ॥ ५१ ॥
म्हणे यांसी नेऊं किंवा प्राण देऊं । उपोषणें बहु आरंभिलीं ॥ ५२ ॥
सात दीन जेव्हां उदकही न घे । पांडुरंगमाय बोले तेव्हां ॥ ५३ ॥
येके दिसीं मज नेई अनेगोंदीं । आणीकही संधी ऐक येक ॥ ५४ ॥
माझीया संतांचा होतां अपमान । तात्काळ तेथोन येईन मी ॥ ५५ ॥
कबूल करोनी नेलें कैसें ऐका । मनुष्येंचि देखा उभीं केलीं ॥ ५६ ॥
बहु प्रेत्नें नेले देव अनेगोंदीं । करी पूजाविधि मनोभावें ॥ ५७ ॥
भानुदास संत तेथें गेले जेव्हां । अपमान तेव्हां केला रायें ॥ ५८ ॥
कळतांचि संत नेत्रां आले अश्रु । म्हणे सर्वेश्वरु जातो आतां ॥ ५९ ॥
पांडुरंग राया म्हणती आमुची भाक । उगवली देख जाऊं आतां ॥ ६० ॥
आमुचो प्रतिमा करोनी बैसवी । मजऐसे भावी संत माझे ॥ ६१ ॥
राव म्हणे येका दिसांतचि जावें । मग देवरावें मान्य केलें ॥ ६२ ॥
भानुदासें देवा उचलोनी घेतलें । तळ्यामाजीं नेलें अकस्मात ॥ ६३ ॥
जाला गुप्त चंद्रभागेंत निघाला । जयजयकार जाला पंढरीसी ॥ ६४ ॥
आणीयला देव धन्य संतराव । भानुदासा सर्व नमना येती ॥ ६५ ॥
पंढरीचा राव पंढरीस आला । आनंद जाहाला यात्रेलागीं ॥ ६६ ॥
कथेचा विस्तार आहेच बहुत । भीमें संकळित वर्णीयलें ॥ ६७ ॥

॥ इति श्रीभानुदास आख्यान संपूर्ण ॥ शुभं भवतु ॥

Appendix VI

परिशिष्ट ६.

एकनाथी भागवत.

अध्याय १ ला---ओंव्या १३१-१३४.

वंदूं भानुदास आतां ॥ जो कां पितामहाचा पिता
ज्याचेनि वंश भगवंता ॥ झाला सर्वथा प्रियकर ॥ १३१ ॥

जेणें बाळपणीं आकळिला भानु ॥ स्वयें झाला चिद्भानु
जिंतोनि मानाभिमानु ॥ भगवत्पावनू स्वयें झाला ॥ १३२ ॥

जयाची पदबंधप्राप्ती ॥ पाहों आली श्रीविठ्ठलमूर्ती
कानींचीं कुंडलें जगा ज्योती ॥ करितां रातीं देखिला ॥ १३३ ॥

तया भानुदासाचा चक्रपाणी ॥ तयाचाही सुत सुलक्षणी
तयासी सूर्यनाम ठेवूनी ॥ निर्जी निज होऊनी भानुदास ठेला ॥ १३४ ॥